WALLACE LOCKHART's life is dominated by music and writing. He has scripted ten musical journeys which focus on Scottish literary figures and aspects of Scottish life. He has compered international dance festivals and taken part in many musical events in the UK and overseas with his music group Quern.

Away from his word processor or music stand, Wallace Lockhart admits to a love of black labradors, canoeing, walking Scotland's hills and reading the verse of Robert Service.

By the same author:
Highland Balls and Village Halls (Luath Press)
Fiddles and Folk (Luath Press)
On the Trail of Robert Service (Luath Press)
The Scots and Their Oats (Birlinn)
The Scots and Their Fish (Birlinn)

The
Scottish Wedding Book

G.W. LOCKHART

Luath Press Limited

EDINBURGH

www.luath.co.uk

First published 2002
Reprinted 2004

The paper used in this book is acid-free, neutral-sized and recyclable.
It is made from low-chlorine pulps produced in a low-energy,
low-emission manner from renewable forests.

Printed and bound by
Bell & Bain Ltd, Glasgow

Designed by Tom Bee, Edinburgh

Wedding dress illustrations by Jane Smith
Kilt illustration by Jim Coltman

Typeset in Sabon and Frutiger by
Helen Johnston, Berwick-upon-Tweed

To Ailie, Sophie and Emmie

By night, by day, a-field, at hame,
The thoughts of thee my breast inflame;
And ay I muse and sing thy name,
I only live to love thee.

Tho' I were doomed to wander on,
Beyond the sea, beyond the sun;
Till my last, weary sand was run, –
Till then – and then I love thee!

From O, *Were I on Parnassus Hill*
ROBERT BURNS

Acknowledgements

WHILE I HAVE HAD MY SHARE OF weddings from all points of the compass, if I can put it that way, I have found the writing of *The Scottish Wedding Book* made both easier and more exhilarating by the interest shown in it by a wide range of friends, colleagues and worthies. It would be both impolite and unappreciative of me not to make due acknowledgement.

My thanks go to Rev. Ian Paterson and Father Pat Boyan, both of Linlithgow, Rev. Alex Cairns of Sandhead and Rev. Duncan McCosh of Falkirk (I am grateful to them for keeping me on the straight and narrow with regard to many of my facts, and also for putting the odd story in my direction), and to Rev. David Ogston; to Heather Knox for jogging my memory about so many things and to Amy Donaldson of Quern for nit-picking over the drafts of the dances; to Lynda Denton of Gretna Museum and Tourist Services for her valuable information; to organist and choirmaster Andrew Sutherland, and to Paul Bradford of Paul Bradford Designer Cakes, Linlithgow, who introduced me to the fascinating world of cake design. I acknowledge too the help given by staff of New Register House, Edinburgh, and I express my indebtedness to Margaret King of Angus Council Cultural Services.

I express totally inadequate thanks to Jane Smith of Belmont Bridal Studios of Aberdeen. Without her willingness to put her classic good taste and immense knowledge at my disposal, this book would be much less than complete.

Extract from *A Skinful of Scotch* by Cliff Hanley reproduced with permission of Curtis Brown Ltd, London, on behalf of Mr Clifford Hanley; copyright Mr Clifford Hanley. *Maid o' the Mill* by Charles Murray reproduced by kind permission of Charles Murray Memorial Fund, c/o Stronachs Solicitors, Aberdeen. Extracts from *The New Testament in Scots* by W.L. Lorimer and edited by Robin Lorimer, first published as a Canongate Classic in 2001 by, and reproduced by kind permission of, Canongate Books Ltd, Edinburgh; copyright R.L.C. Lorimer. 'The Merriage Service in Scots' including The Twenty-Third Psalm of King Dauvit and The Lord's Prayer translated by, and reproduced by kind permission of, Rev. David Ogston of St John's Kirk, Perth; copyright D. Ogston.

Contents

DRESSING FOR YOUR WEDDING DAY: THE GROOM

DRESSING FOR YOUR WEDDING DAY: THE BRIDE

Preface

'ALL THE WORLD LOVES A LOVER', runs the old saying. Though casual dress holds sway, the Scot likes to appear in all his or her finery when the wedding bells toll. But it is not just finery that makes a Scottish wedding so distinctive: there is an added urge to bring to the surface that something in our veins that makes us Scots. And we express it in, amongst other things, our national dress and our music and dance. What better outlet is there than a wedding to be at home with traditions?

In this book I have tried, by travelling the centuries, to show how weddings have developed in our land. There are one or two surprises.

For practical advice on the necessary arrangements and the duties of individuals on the day I have spoken to ministers, priests and registrars, and not a few of those who have been through the marriage mill. In our land of contrasts, inevitably there is an abundance of local variation, but that is both the price and the bonus of being a Scot. One recognises, though, the increasing easing of formalities at weddings – for example, the mingling of the two sides in the church before the ceremony, instead of the traditional 'his side and her side'.

The dances of Scotland have, as some readers may know from my previous books, long been an interest of mine. I have concentrated here on those dances particularly appropriate to a wedding reception, recognising there will be some in attendance who may not have been on the floor for some time, if at all.

When I came to write the section on dress, I was reminded in terms ranging from the ungallant to the politically incorrect that I was in big trouble should I devote more space to the wedding finery of the groom than to that of his wife-to-be. That raised a problem. I recognise a well-dressed woman when I see one, but the thought of giving advice on female wedding dress was enough to send shivers up my spine and a few other places besides. But there are horses for courses, and I am indeed fortunate that Jane Smith of Belmont Bridal Studios in Aberdeen, one of Scotland's foremost figures in bridalwear, came to my rescue. To Jane I am grateful for ensuring no suggestion of bias or chauvinism can now be laid at my door.

I hope this book will both entertain and enlighten. It is good to know something of the past as we go forward. To those approaching that special day I pass on the old country toast:

May the best you've ever seen
Be the worst you'll ever see,
May the moose ne'er leave your girnal
Wi' a rear drop in its een.
May ye aye be hale and hearty
Till ye'r auld enough to dee,
May ye aye be just as happy
As I wish ye aye to be.

Why Get Married In Scotland?

WHY GET MARRIED IN SCOTLAND? Why indeed get married anywhere else? The case for getting married in Scotland is overwhelming, so let us take a minute or two to consolidate making one's wedding a truly Scottish affair.

The blood that flows through the veins of a Scot is rich in love for his or her native land, a love that lingers even though years and miles may separate the person from what they know to be their homeland. As the old *Canadian Boat Song* puts it:

> From the lone sheiling of the misty island,
> Mountains divide us, and a waste of sea;
> Yet still the blood is strong; the heart is highland,
> And we in dreams behold the Hebrides.

Leading up to their wedding day, in most cases the most important day of one's life, many Scots feel an urge that defies description to be at home with their roots. Today we see the increasing number of couples of Scottish stock arriving from overseas to pledge their troth to each other. In some cases, we must admit, the Scottish link is but tenuous.

Weddings, of course, are based on romance, and who is going to deny Scotland is a romantic country? No need to dwell on such figures as Bonnie Prince Charlie, Flora Macdonald, Rob Roy or the Border Reivers. The very fabric of the country opens like a book to those hearts susceptible to history and tradition, who respond to the call of the pipes and the glamour of our national dress. And while there is worldwide recognition that Scotland's scenery is incomparable, there is now also acknowledgement of the numerous and diverse places, from historic houses to simple outdoor locations, where the wedding ceremony can be performed. This is not to direct attention away from churches. Many will wish to maintain their link with their local church on their wedding day and there is something impressive about the Scottish wedding ceremony being performed in its traditional setting. The seriousness of the vows seems to be emphasised in the silence of a Scottish kirk.

The ceremony over, Scottish traditions have a full part to play. The newly weds may be piped into the reception where a clarsach brings charm and dignity behind the buzz of conversation.

Marriage is that relation between man and a woman in which independence is equal, the dependence is mutual, and the obligation is reciprocal. (Louis Kaufman Arspacloz)

For the toast a good dram will be welcomed by many and at the table salmon and venison may be served, or the time-honoured ham or steak pie. Cheeses from Orkney to Ayrshire will be found to be fitting companions, while Scotch trifle and cranachan are worthy contenders for heavenly accolades.

After the reception comes the honeymoon and in Scotland one is spoilt for choice. For the truly romantic the call may come from the remoteness of South Uist or the Highland reaches of Sutherland. Those who want to combine country and town may see Perthshire or Deeside as their haven. The physically active might give thought to the hiring of a cabin cruiser on the Caledonian Canal, joining a yacht on an island-hopping holiday, or consider marrying while on a skiing holiday in the Cairngorms. An obvious honeymoon choice is to be pampered in a luxury hotel, either in the country or in a centre such as Edinburgh with easy access to theatres, concerts and a host of interesting places. Or you could tour, preferably with an agenda, such as playing over Scotland's leading golf courses.

A honeymoon is very special and requires as much thought as the rest of the wedding arrangements. Scotland offers a home to all options.

The Wedding Story

If doughty deeds my ladye please,
Right soon I'll mount my steed;
And strong his arm, and fast his seat,
That bears frae me the meed.
I'll wear thy colours in my cap,
The picture in my heart;
And he that bends not to thine eye,
Shall rue it to his smart.

Then tell me how to woo thee, love;
O tell me how to woo thee!
For thy dear sake, nae care I'll take,
Tho' ne'er another trow me.
If gay attire delight thine eye,
I'll dight me in array;
I'll tend thine chamber door all night,
And squire thee all the day.
If sweetest sounds can win thy ear,
These sounds I'll strive to catch;
Thy voice I'll steal to woo thysel',
That voice that none can match.

But if fond love thy heart can gain,
I never broke a vow;
Nae maiden lays her skaith to me,
I never loved but you.
For you alone I ride the ring,
For you I wear the blue;
For you alone I strive to sing,
O tell me how to woo!

O Tell Me How To Woo Thee
ROBERT CUNNINGHAME-GRAHAM OF GARTMORE

The Roots of Today's Ceremony

WEDDINGS ARE AS OLD AS the hills, perhaps even older. Certainly long before Saint Paul was leading with the advice that wives should obey their husbands, blushing brides and excited husbands-to-be were anticipating the living-happily-ever-after routine. And, for just as long, the tying of the knot was the excuse for a celebration. And why not? A wedding is a happy event. If a couple can't enjoy their wedding when surrounded by friends and family, then the outlook is bleak.

It is in Roman times that we first really recognise the roots of today's wedding ceremony and all that goes with it. Consent was needed from the head of the family, *paterfamilias*, before a marriage could take place, a ring was given at the time of betrothal, the married couple were showered with almonds (the precursor of confetti) as an expressed hope of fertility, and, as the wine miracle at Canna confirmed, wedding-time was also party-time.

Columba arrived on Iona in the sixth century, bringing Christianity to Scotland and, presumably, a Christian approach to marriage. This early form of Christianity of course followed the Roman Catholic persuasion, appropriate guidance and edict being issued from time to time by the Pope of the day. Early Christian marriages apparently did not need the presence of a priest, a promise of marriage making the whole thing respectable. Things got tidied up a bit in the thirteenth century when Pope Innocent III instituted the 'calling of banns', so giving time for any objections to be raised. It is interesting to note that this practice – which involved ministers declaring 'purposes of marriage' from the pulpit in the Church of Scotland on a Sunday morning, to the accompaniment of heads wagging up and down or shaken dolefully from side to side depending on the perceived suitability of the marriage – continued in Scotland until 1977. But quite incredibly, the legal age for marriage in Scotland until 1929 was 12 for women and 14 for men, so perhaps the 'calling of banns' made more than a little sense.

While marriages up to the time of Malcolm Canmore in the latter half of the eleventh century might have been happy events for those with status, the humble serf was not so lucky. Being devoid of rights and privileges, he was unable to enter into a contract of marriage. Worse than that, as former Secretary of State Tom Johnston points out in his *History of the Scottish Working Classes*, the lord of the soil could, under Mercheta Mulierum, claim possession of a female serf for the first night after her marriage. What the lord's wife might have had to say about that is not known, but it is understandable that the only way a handsome working-class bride could escape spending her marriage night at the castle was to postpone her wedding until she became a mother.

Over the centuries the church worked hard to bring order to marrying but we Scots, being possessors of a cussed streak, inevitably supported arrangements that suited ourselves, frequently basing the tying of a knot around the couple stating their free consent to marry each other. As an old book puts it:

> If a man and woman have lived together as husband and wife, and have had the uncontradicted reputation among their neighbours of being married to one another, these parties will be held to have exchanged a consent to marry, and the courts will declare them to be married.

While this marriage by habit and repute may have been a variation of today's common-law marriage (the phrase 'bidie-in' has long been in the Scots language), it was a good example of Scottish canniness with the pennies. A wedding yesteryear, as today, made a big hole in the bank account.

Handfasting

Trial marriages are not a new invention. To the couple unsure of their ground, the old custom of handfasting proved a popular expedient. Handfasting has a long history capable of being traced back to the 1500s. In its earliest form it was like an engagement, an expressed intention of becoming man and wife by the physical contact of 'hands on fist'. From that simple act it developed into a trial marriage scheduled to last for a year and a day. When that time was up the couple were then obliged to get married properly or go their separate ways, no stigma being attached to the latter action.

The kirk sessions regarded themselves as 'watchmen ower Christ's flok' – watchmen with special instructions against sparing the rod. They put down the old system of hand-fast marriages whereby men and women contracted themselves on trial to each other for a year and a day before going to the priest for official ratification of the marriage. (From History of the Working Classes in Scotland, *Tom Johnston)*

There was probably a practical reason for the development of handfasting. In certain communities, such as the crofting and fishing communities, there was a need for a wife to produce sons and daughters capable of contributing to the husband's occupation. Handfasting allowed an exploration of fertility. Any child produced during the handfasting period was recognised as legitimate. If the couple decided not to get married at the end of the period, any child of theirs appears to have become the responsibility of the partner opposing a marriage – a subtle way of exerting pressure, although in some parts of the country such offspring seem automatically to have been given to the father for care at the end of the year. The practical aspect of handfasting is further emphasised by the fact that most arrangements were entered into at Lammas Fair time when country folk would gather together to pay their rent. Martin Martin, traveller to the Western Isles, wrote in 1695 that 'the unreasonable custom of handfasting was long ago brought into disuse.' Perhaps not so long ago on the mainland, as the Statistical Account for Eskdale, written a century later, suggests:

> That piece of ground at the meeting of the Black and White Esks was remarkable in former times; remarkable for an annual fair where it was the custom for unmarried persons of both sexes to choose a companion with whom they were to live until that time next year. This was called handfasting or hand-in-fist. If they were pleased with each other at that time, then they continued for life; if not they separated, and were free to make another choice as at the first. The fruit of their connection (if there were any) was always attached to the disaffected person. In later times, when this part of the country belonged to the Abbacy of Melrose, a priest (to whom they gave the name of 'Book i bosom', either because he carried in his bosom a Bible, or perhaps a register of the marriages) came from time to time to confirm the marriages.

Handfasting lingered on in fishing communities and there is a record of a marriage contract with a year-and-a-day clause being entered into in Fraserburgh as late as January 1858, the pregnant, and no doubt happy, lady becoming a fully fledged bride in the November of that year.

Penny Weddings

It goes without saying that the Church, especially as the staunch Presbyterians came to the fore, did not endorse handfasting. By the eighteenth century, marriage had become a more formalised affair. Some Kirk Sessions in a burst of enthusiasm laid down qualifications for entry into marriage, such as the ability to recite the Lord's Prayer and the giving of an assurance that there would be regular attendance at church. Following this a formal contract of marriage might be drawn up. In contrary fashion, the all-clear to get married was an occasion for celebration, and with drink to the fore trouble was frequently not far behind. To alleviate this problem, Sessions might stipulate that contracts of marriage should not be entered into on a Saturday lest a hangover inhibit church attendance the following day.

Expense at a wedding has always been a problem and the answer of the poorer folk, at one time to satisfy the need for food, drink and dancing, was to hold a penny wedding.

Many will have seen original paintings or prints of a penny wedding, sometimes known as a 'penny bridal'. The event was based on an open house approach, anyone being able to attend, even those who were strangers to the bride or groom, so long as they made a contribution to the wedding, usually but not necessarily in cash. Frequently, such weddings were profitable events, the newly weds finishing up with a surplus that would help them get started in married life. These weddings became so popular, and some astute brides so commercially minded as to charge for the ale on tap, that local Justices of the Peace might lay down rules as to allowed levels of expenditure. The number of people arriving at such 'houlies' and the drunkenness and fighting which became part and parcel of the penny wedding eventually forced the church to become involved, though with some restraint. Anne Gordon in *Candie For The Foundling* sets out the awkward situation in which the church found itself. It had to recognise that a rowdy wedding was still an improvement on a couple living in sin:

> As the kirk gradually had more opportunity to turn its mind to such matters, its opinion of penny weddings became less and less favourable, with one Presbytery saying that 'as a result of going to them many people "fell a sacrifice to lust and luxury and some loose persons usually frequenting these occasions, do by the influence of their bad example embolden others to sin"'. But even when the General Assembly passed an Act against penny bridals in 1645, describing them as 'fruitful seminaries of all lasciviousness and debaucherie' it still did not seek to stop them but just to restrain abuses at them.

This reasonable approach from the church had little influence and further attempts over the years still had little effect. Even as late as the 1790s we can read of their popularity, in the Statistical Account for the parish of Avoch:

> Most marriages of that date took the form of penny weddings with bread, ale and whisky provided in the house and dancing going on in a barn to the music of a fiddler or two, all of which was kept up for two or three days until the Saturday night. The couple then went to church on Sunday and on their return gave a dinner or similar form of entertainment, all of which was done with little loss or gain to them.

Weddings easily become boisterous affairs and it would seem the only complaint against penny weddings was that there was no guest list – anyone was welcome. The idea of making a contribution to costs need not repel. One of the big differences between weddings today and yesteryear is that, as we shall see later, in earlier times friends and relatives had a greater involvement in all the preparations. Weddings where families and friends made a contribution in money or kind continued, certainly amongst poorer people, well into the twentieth century, and any outsider attempting to gatecrash these events would have been given short shrift.

Not all couples were in a position to let their hair down at the time of their marriage. When a couple faced strong family disapproval, one answer was to elope, an action that has found much favour in Scotland and England over the years. Chambers in his *Traditions of Edinburgh,* which looks at life in the capital in the 1700s, notes:

> A large room in the White Horse Inn in Boyd's Close, Canongate, was the frequent scene of the marriages of runaway English couples, at a time when these irregularities were permitted in Edinburgh.

The most famous venue for runaway marriages, of course, is Gretna Green, on the border with England, where a so-called Anvil priest performed the ceremony in the blacksmith's shop. While most couples getting married there today (legally, in the presence of a minister or a registrar) are Scots, we have to thank an English lord for creating the reputation of this most unlikely wedding venue.

Elopement

In the 1700s there seems to have been much greater concern in England than in Scotland about the virtues or otherwise of irregular marriages, as such marriages outwith the church's authority were known, and in 1754 Lord Hardwick was a happy man as he saw his Marriage Act passed by Parliament. In brief, the Act stated the marriage ceremony had to take place in a church and that both parties had to be at least 21 years of age. Scotland, with its own legal system, was naturally not interested in providing succour to the noble lord, and ignored the leglislation, so opening a welcoming door for those prevented from marrying in England because they were under 21 or were lacking parental approval. Such couples in love took the high road north, stopping at Gretna, the first village on 'the right side of the Border'. Thomas Pennant in his 1772 *Tour of Scotland and Voyage to the Hebrides* had this to say:

> . . . stop at the little village of Gretna, the resort of all amorous couples, whose union the prudence of parents or guardians prohibits; here the young pair may be instantly united by a fisherman, a joiner, or a blacksmith, who marry from two guineas a job to a dram of whisky: but the price is generally adjusted by the information of the postilions from Carlisle, who are in pay of one or other of the above worthies; but even the drivers, in case of necessity, have been known to undertake the sacerdotal office. If the pursuit of friends proves very hot, and there is not time for the ceremony, the frightened pair are advised to slip into bed; are shown to the pursuers, who imagining they are irrevocably united, retire and leave them to 'consummate their unfinished loves'. The Church of Scotland does what it can to prevent these clandestine matches; but in vain, for these infamous couplers despise the fulmination of the Kirk, and excommunication is the only penalty it can inflict.

Let it not be said the local Scots were slow to see a commercial opportunity. If people wanted to be married, there were plenty of locals willing to provide a couple of witnesses and the necessary service for a guinea or two. And so the local blacksmith's shop came into being as a wedding parlour. There are many extraordinary tales told about runaway couples being pursued north by an irate father with pistol in hand. As the old song had it:

> Oh gallop along with a right merry song,
> Through wood and vale and hollow,
> The turnpike men may shake their heads
> And half the world may follow;
> But I care not what the old folks say
> I'll take no heed or warning,
> For I'll be wearing a wedding ring,
> At Gretna Green in the morning.

What is surprising is the range of people from the south who made for the blacksmith's shop. They covered the entire social field. The Earl of Westmoreland arrived with his sweetheart Sarah Anne Child after her father, a director of Child's Bank, had shot one of their horses. One noble lord, not wishing to be recognised, arrived dressed as a woman. John Peel, the famous huntsman with his bonny Mary White, was another who made the journey to the blacksmith's shop. The marriage trade reached such a booming stage after one Carlisle 'Hiring Day', when it is said 50 couples, no doubt at various levels of intoxication, arrived ready and willing to take the plunge, that some controlling legislation had to be introduced. It came in the form of a 'cooling off' Act which stipulated one of the parties had to be resident in Scotland for 21 days before a marriage could take place. This had the intended effect and the flow of runaway couples slowed down considerably. This represented a partial victory for the Church which had always opposed these Anvil weddings. Ongoing religious pressure resulted in a further Act of Parliament being passed in 1940 stating that weddings had to take place either in a church or in a registry office. This brought the shutters down on the blacksmith's shop, though such was the lure of Gretna Green that many couples made for its registry office to be married.

This, however, was not to be the end of the story. In 1979, both the above Acts were repealed and a few years later the blacksmith's shop was again in business, this time with a difference. Nowadays, the ceremony is legal in every way. As an observer, I have to say I was impressed by the overall ambience that prevails at an Anvil ceremony. The old blacksmith's cottage which adjoins the 'smiddy' has now been turned into a museum. It is perhaps less than surprising that the old blacksmith's shop and its accompanying visitor centre is today second only to Edinburgh Castle in terms of visitor attendance numbers in Scotland. And perhaps we Scots should remind ourselves, as Sir Walter Scott did, that we also did the odd bit of cross-the-Border maurading for wedding purposes:

> The kirk was deck'd at morning tide,
> The tapers glimmer'd fair;
> The priest and bridegroom wait the bride,
> And dame and knight are there:
> They sought her baith by bower and ha';
> The ladie was not seen!
> She's ower the Border, and awa'
> Wi' Jock of Hazeldean.

Bundling and Wooing

If elopement meant excitement, one wonders what word to use to describe the emotions associated with the old custom of 'bundling', an attempt to reconcile passion with respectability. In a world where life was dominated by long hours of work, wooing was essentially a night-time occupation where understanding parents had a part to play. On cold windswept nights, long before the back seats of cars were even a thought, the suitor might have to make a long trek to the house of the girl he wanted to marry, where a large family would be gathered together in the one room; not a happy environment in which to woo. But adjoining the one room with its warming fire was the girl's cold and probably unlit sleeping quarters and to these she retired to keep cosy under a blanket. Enter then her mother who would see that the girl's legs were inserted into a large stocking or sack, which would then be tied securely at the top. Then, in the knowledge that her chastity was secure, the young man was allowed to join her.

On moonlight nights they held their favourite meetings in barn or cottage, called 'Rockings' when young women brought their rocks and reels, or distaffs and spindles – where young men assembled, and to the accompaniment of the spinning of the wool and flax the song and merriment went round, till the company dispersed and the girls went home escorted by their swains who gallantly carried their rocks over corn-rigs and moors.
(From Social Life of Scotland in the Eighteenth Century, *Henry Grey Graham)*

Not all suitors, of course, followed this genteel path, and night wooing, then as now, had its adherents. In 1868 a witness appearing before the Royal Commission on Marriage Laws testified that:

> It was against custom for a lover to visit his sweetheart by day. As to the parents, their daughters must have husbands and there is no other way of courting.

This, of course, was right up Burns' street, as he makes clear in *She Rose And Let Me In*:

> We wedded and concealed our crime,
> Then all was weel again,
> An' now she blesses the happy night
> She rose an' loot me in.

And in *Wha Is That At My Bower Door*:

> In my bower if ye should stay
> Let me stay, quo' Findlay;
> I fear ye'll bide till break of day,
> Indeed will I, quo' Findlay.

Perhaps times haven't changed all that much.

Rings

Rings have a long history of being more than just ornaments. Ancient rings carried engraved signets and early ring-lore is mixed up with the development of seal engraving. Even in the Book of Genesis we read of rings being given as a pledge. And it would appear that wedding rings were worn by Jews prior to Christian times. The Romans considered the giving of a

A Greek fourth-century betrothal ring bears the inscription 'To her who excels not only in virtue and prudence, but also in wisdom'.

ring as part of a betrothal and we can trace back to the Middle Ages the giving of betrothal rings in Scotland, normally of silver and known as a 'fede' ring. This was a distinctive and recognisable ring because part of it was made up of a clasped-hand emblem. We can assume silver rings were more common than gold ones due to the scarcity of gold in Scotland. Ruddiman in his *Introduction to Anderson's Diplomata* claims that gold was almost never seen in Scotland, most of it going abroad to pay for imported goods. However, Burt in his *Letters From the North of Scotland*, written in the early 1700s, comments, 'they do not use the ring in marriage, as in England.' So we have the suggestion of different practices ruling in the Highlands and the Lowlands. Anne Gordon in *Candie For The Foundling* describes the use of a ring as security that a wedding would go ahead:

> In 1630 a couple came to the Kirk Session of the Canongate Kirk in Edinburgh and gave up their names to be proclaimed, and consigned ane gold signet ring. This being in Episcopalian times, this choice of pledge may have been because in most Episcopalian churches, rings are regarded as symbols of pledges or contracts.

Not always was the betrothal present a ring; there are examples of more useful adornments such as snuff-boxes being given. An essentially Scottish gift was the Luckenbooth brooch. As street market stalls gave way to booths that could be locked up at night for security, the first such premises, especially on Edinburgh's Royal Mile, were occupied by silversmiths and goldsmiths. The most famous of these was George Heriot (known as 'Jingling Geordie' because of his habit of playing with money in his pocket), who would entertain his monarch in his seven-by-seven-foot booth. These craftsmen pro-duced the heart-shaped brooch normally topped with a crown design that is still made today and is one of our most delightful expressions of love. Certainly they were in existence long before the jewelled, often diamond, engagement ring used today made its first appearance, possibly towards the end of the nineteenth century.

The use of the wedding ring among Christians can be traced back to 860 AD when a marriage settlement was properly sealed. Rings bearing the names of the newly married couple were passed round guests for inspection. As the third finger of the left hand was believed to be directly connected to the vena amoris, the vein of love, the ring was placed there.

One old custom was for the bride to be given two rings, the less expensive one being used when the wife was undertaking physi-cal work, so safeguarding the main and more expensive ring.

Another fairly recent innovation is the eternity ring, when a doting husband may express his feelings after some years of mar-ried bliss. A common and fairly recently instituted practice is for the bride, as well as receiving a ring, to give the groom a wedding ring, and this giving and receiving takes place as the minister, in a church wedding, utters the well-known words:

By this sign you take each other, to have and to hold from this day forward, for better, for worse; for richer, for poorer; in sickness and in health; to love and to cherish, till death do you part.

It really is a pretty serious obligation.

It is the accepted practice to place the wedding ring on the third finger of the left hand, possibly because this finger is supposed to be linked directly through a vein to the heart. In the past other fingers have been used, including the thumb in England in Elizabethan times. One suspects a connection between a ring and the Celtic expression of eternity as expressed in a chain or Celtic cross, but the proof is sketchy.

Wedding Traditions

Various communities often had their own ways of celebrating the coming together of a couple. The fishing communities provide a prime example of this, although nowadays, with fishermen often finding brides from outwith the fishing world, the old traditions have weakened to an extent. Many such weddings, for example, would be set to take place in the winter months when hard seas restricted fishing, and there seems to have been a relationship between the size of catches and matrimony. If the catches were good, wedding bells would ring; if not, the fishermen appeared to have lost the notion.

There was often a ritual attached to the prospective groom seeking the girl's hand. Known as 'the Speerin' or 'the Beukin', it involved the bride's father feigning displeasure, making the suitor sweat a bit before giving his consent. That hurdle over, the minister would be asked to make the appropriate proclamation from the pulpit. Then followed 'the Biddin' when virtually the whole community would be given a spoken invitation by the best man and maid (and the now obsolete worst man and worst maid) to attend. Wedding clothes were now bought, the bride more likely to choose a coloured dress than a white one, and there was a fondness for a Paisley shawl or a Paisley-patterned dress.

The wild carrot has long borne a symbolic reputation for human fruitfulness in the Gaelic world and, in the West Highlands particularly, the Sunday before St Michael's Day, which falls on 29 September, was known as Carrot Sunday, or Domhnach Curran. On that day girls would present their intended husbands small bunches of carrots tied with a red ribbon. When Saint Michael's Day itself arrived, it was given over to much music-making and such dances as the Cath na Coilleach and Cailleach an Dudain which portray the virility of the Gael.

One of the main differences between today's expensive affair and the wedding of yesteryear is that there was formerly greater community involvement. The best man had much more to do than make a speech: he was involved in helping to organise the cleaning and whitewashing of the house, while the best maid would join other ladies as they made pillows and bolsters and other things for the house. These functions were carried out to the accompaniment of music and singing and were regarded very much as part of the wedding. The receiving of crockery from neighbours was an important event as in some fishing villages status was attached to the number of jugs received to be put on show. In the main, the groom supplied the table and chairs for the new home, the bride contributing the bed.

As elsewhere in the country, 'the feet washing' was an important prelude to the wedding ceremony, and this could be done to the bride and groom separately or together. While a certain amount of decorum might surround the washing of the bride's feet, the groom would not be so lucky. Out would come the blackening or soot and revelry was the order of the day. Soot, of course, has long figured in wedding celebrations, it being believed at one time to possess magical properties because of its connection with fire and hearth.

A tradition which still lingers in places like Shetland is the walking in procession to the place of the wedding ceremony, be it church or manse or hall. In more superstitious times, guns would be fired to ward off evil spirits, although a kirk session in the town of Banchory in 1732 fined two enthusiastic guests for the over-exuberant firing of their muskets. Veils were not just for adornment, they were intended as a distraction to confuse unkind spirits by making identification of the bride difficult. A fiddler or piper would lead the way and there might be the odd stop on the walk for a refreshment.

There are, of course, many local wedding traditions and practices that never make the headlines. St Cyrus in Kincardineshire provides a good example. To this village in 1843 retired one John

Orr from the Madras Civil Service. Seeing a newly married couple come out from the church one stormy day, he was so moved by their plight and thoughts of what the future might hold for them that he bequeathed money to the church to allow a payment to be made every year to the tallest, shortest, oldest and youngest bride being married in the parish. Since that time, the vital statistic, if I can use that term, has been verified after every wedding ceremony. The good man's generosity has now, though, become a matter for debate. Competition has decreased; the village seldom sees more than four weddings in a year.

Nowadays, with couples taking off for a honeymoon after the wedding ceremony, the old tradition of the 'Beddin' or 'Hystin' is no longer practised, and it is maybe just as well. It left little to the imagination as friends helped the newly married couple into bed on their first night. A variation seems to have existed in parts of the Highlands, as Burt points out:

> When a young couple are married, on the first night the company keep possession of the dwelling-house, giving them straw, heath, or fern for a bed, with blankets for their covering; and then they make merry, and dance to the piper all the night long.

Other communities and towns have had or still have their own ways of acknowledging weddings. I remember well how the jute mill girls in Dundee would dress up in net curtains a girl getting married and boisterously wheel her up and down the streets in a barrow.

A favourite Dundee joke used to be: 'Are you a spinster?' asked the registrar; 'Na, eh'm a weaver' replied the mill girl. Mary Brooksbank, who interpreted Dundee mill life like few others, would sing:

> Oh the gaffer's looking worried
> An' the flett's a' in a steer,

Jessie Brodie's gettin' married,
In the morn sh'll no' be here.

They bocht a cheeny tea set,
An a chanty fu' o' saut,
A bonnie coloured carpet,
A kettle and a pot.

The appearance of a chanty, or chamber pot, and salt was not confined to Dundee. Margaret Bennet in her *Scottish Customs From Cradle to Grave* tells how a girl to be married in Kilmarnock would be dressed up in coloured paper flowers and required to jump a salt-filled chanty, probably in a main street, in which colleagues had slipped in money and articles associated with a wedding night. Salt, of course, has long been associated in Scotland with prosperity and plenty. An old tradition which has been revived in recent years is the decision by many brides to maintain their own surname after marriage. A stroll through an old graveyard will often show this was common practice until around the middle of the nineteenth century. Few things are ever new. Creeping in today is the decision by some brides to hyphenate their surname with that of their husband.

Finally, a comment about timing. June has always been the most popular month for weddings, May the least popular. 'Marry in May and rue the day' goes the old rhyme and we know that after Mary Queen of Scots married the Earl of Bothwell on 15 May 1567, various lines about ill-omened women marrying in May were attached to the gates of Holyrood Palace. The moon, too, especially in the North East, might warrant consideration, it being thought a good omen if it is increasing in size, while a waning moon is a bad omen for the bride's future happiness:

A growing moon and a flowing tide
Fortune smiles on the happy bride.

As to the selection of day, such choices that have been put into verse are contradictory, as the following will show:

Monday for health / *Monday for wealth*
Tuesday for wealth / *Tuesday for health*
Wednesday best day of all / *Wednesday no luck at all*
Thursday for curses
Friday for crosses / *Friday for losses*
Saturday no luck at all / *Saturday best day of all*

Your Wedding

. . . but I hope my dear Eliza, you will do
me the justice to believe me, when I assure
you the love I have for you is founded on
the sacred principles of virtue and honour,
and in consequence so long as you continue
to be possessed of these amiable qualities
which first inspired my passion for you, so
long must I continue to love you. Believe
me, my dear, it is love like this alone which
can render the marriage state happy. People
may talk of flames and raptures as long as
they please, and a warm fancy, with a flow
of youthful spirits, may make them feel
something like what they describe; but sure
I am the nobler faculties of the mind with
kindred feelings of the heart can only be the
foundation of friendship, and it has always
been my opinion that the married life was
only friendship in a more exalted degree.

From *On Love and Marriage*
ROBERT BURNS

Introduction

WHAT MAKES TODAY'S WEDDING different? How will social historians interpret our attitudes towards marriage?

Perhaps first and foremost we must recognise that today's bride and groom have a few more years to their credit as they walk down the aisle than was common in earlier times. The average age for marrying today is around 30 and this has a distinct bearing on the wedding arrangements. Generally, more money will be available for an exotic honeymoon, the expensive location for a reception is not such a frightening factor and inevitably the couple will have had more exposure to good living. Their expectations in terms of food and service will be higher; they will have experienced more sophistication and be more comfortable with it than yesteryear's younger bride. And hopefully these extra years will make them more capable of resolving the niggles and problems that even the best of marriages must cope with.

This added maturity at nuptial time will mean the bride and groom are likely to be further up the career ladder and more aware of what the world has to offer. This encourages more lateral thinking about how the wedding day should be structured. The commercial world has not been slow in coming to their aid. Advisers to ensure the important day goes as it should offer their services, wedding shows, magazines, cake and ring designers, video producers and venue providers are all eager to make their contribution. Never before have weddings been such big business. And the Scottish emphasis is there for everyone to see. It has been estimated that over 80 per cent of today's grooms wear the kilt, brides are turning to Celtic designs, and heritage buildings are providing more and more wedding venues. This is no mere hark back to the past. Everything to do with a wedding is concerned with the future. The words of an old Gaelic poem come to mind:

She stood in her snood and arisaid
Beneath the trees of the wood,
The buckled plaid round her shoulder laid,
She looked for him as she stood.

He came to her running o'er the heath,
A present was in his hand,
And upon his dirk drawn from the sheath
They plighted their troth to stand.

O God give the joy and God the love
To those who are lovers true,
Shed down benediction from above
As in one are joined the two.

A Religious or a Civil Ceremony?

THE BLOOD IS COURSING through the veins, the perfect partner has been found, the urge to tie the knot is irresistible. It is time to study the nuts and bolts of where and how to be married. Among the first issues to be resolved is whether the wedding is to be a church or civil affair. A little background information may not go amiss here.

In days gone by, marriages were considered to be either 'regular' or 'irregular', the former involving a minister of religion, the latter coming into the categories of 'habit and repute', 'by promise *subsequente copula*' or '*declaration de presenti*'. Indeed, until 1811 a marriage service anywhere other than in a church was considered irregular and a minister conducting a marriage in a private house could be in big trouble with his presbytery. The Marriage (Scotland) Act of 1939 tidied things up. Henceforth, marriages would be either religious or civil.

A religious wedding conducted by a minister may take place at a location of your choice. Do make sure, though, that the minister is happy to perform the act of worship at your chosen location.

Now, a civil wedding may take place at locations outside of the registry office, so long as that location is licensed for civil weddings.

The 1939 Act stipulated that the religious marriage had to follow the accepted form of the Christian or Jewish faith and made no reference to marriages of those committed to other religions. As our society became more multi-racial, it was clear that a change to legislation was necessary. This was attended to in the 1977 Marriage (Scotland) Act, where, to use the words of the *Church of Scotland Year Book*, 'the benefits of religious marriage have been extended to adherents of other faiths, the only requirements being the observance of monogamy and the satisfaction of the authorities with the forms of the vows imposed.'

Certain common elements are relevant to both types of marriage. For example, the minimum legal age is 16, parental consent not being required. It is necessary that both partners are sufficiently mentally sound to appreciate the nature and obligations of what they are entering into, and are acting by their own consent.

What, then, are the preparatory steps?

First, both parties are obliged to formally advise the registrar in the district where they are to be married of their intention, by completing a marriage notice form. This form is valid for a three-month period. Technically it has to be completed and returned at least 15 days before the date of the wedding but registrars recommend that the form be presented four to six weeks ahead of the date (things can go wrong). This form should be accompanied by birth certificates and proof that any previous marriages have been formally terminated.

In Scotland, the minimum legal age for marriage is 16.

You must obtain and complete a marriage notice form, available from the registrar in the district in which you intend to marry.

Make sure you return this form and all other documentation four to six weeks before the date of your wedding. Your marriage schedule will be prepared from this.

In the case of a religious ceremony, don't forget to take your marriage schedule with you on the big day – you won't be able to marry without it!

After a religious ceremony, the schedule must be returned to the registrar within three days (a friend can do this for you).

While there is no need for a residency qualification to be married in Scotland nowadays, people from elsewhere can have difficulty in proving the formal ending to a previous marriage, for example, if such documents are not available in the English language. It is for such reasons that the early return of the marriage notice form is recommended.

Use is often made of this residency flexibility by couples from outwith Scotland who wish to be married in Scotland. One of the most famous occasions of recent times, of course, was when Madonna, international star and toast of millions, elected to be married at Skibo Castle in Sutherland. Although there was much local excitement and speculation about the appropriateness of a

Highland venue for such a wedding, it has to be said the couple saw to it their visit to Skibo was a sincere affair and were much applauded for their decorum.

One should note, too, the Church of Scotland's tolerance towards the marrying of divorcees, and the great and the good have joined the ordinary man and woman in the street in making use of the Church of Scotland's open-door approach. In recent times Princess Anne remarried in Scotland at Craithie Church on Deeside without, it can be said, scarcely an eyebrow being raised.

It is from the marriage notice form that the registrar prepares the marriage schedule. If it is to be a civil ceremony, the form will be retained by the registrar once it has been signed by the necessary two witnesses.

A Civil Wedding

The civil wedding, which can only take place on approved premises and must be conducted by a registrar in the presence of two witnesses over the age of 16, was introduced in 1854, when an Act of Parliament put the onus on individuals to register such events as marriages, along with births and deaths, with a civil authority. This Act initiated the appointing of registrars in every parish, as well as the establishment of a national Register House. The thinking behind the Act was simply to improve registration by transferring the responsibility from church to state, a duty the church had carried out, inevitably with varying levels of accuracy, for many centuries.

One of the most famous early recorded weddings is the marriage of Mary Queen of Scots to Lord Darnley on 29 July 1565 in the Edinburgh Canongate parish. This was a Sunday wedding, it should be noted – a case of the better the day, the better the deed. These early parish records have been a tremendous boon to those intent on tracing their ancestry.

A Religious Wedding

A religious wedding is more flexible than a civil ceremony. Whilst most Christian weddings take place in a church, and many couples feel they are not properly married unless a church is the venue, they need not do so. There is no Church of Scotland restriction on time or location so long as the proposed arrangement has the sympathy of the minister, who carries the authority to undertake marriages under the Marriage (Scotland) Act 1977.

The way is open for the wedding to be held in locations of special meaning for the prospective bride and groom. University chapels, historic buildings and stately homes hired for the occasion share popularity with marquees and open air locations, hotels and homes.

Where a church wedding is planned, the marriage schedule is still a requirement, but in this instance the schedule must be collected by one of the partners not more than a week before the wedding. It will then be signed by the officiating minister and witnesses during the ceremony and must be returned, within three days, to the registrar.

There is no requirement that a couple wishing to be married in the Church of Scotland be church members, although it is no doubt an item that warrants serious discussion. It is a question the minister is likely to ask if the couple are not known to him. And it is the minister's decision as to whether or not a couple should or should not be married in his or her church. A minister will not usually charge a fee for conducting a wedding service but that does not mean it is a no-cost affair. A donation for the use of the church will certainly be expected to cover overheads such as heating and greater generosity will be expected from non-members than members.

The organist, too, is worthy of his labour, as are the beadle and bell-ringer. Agreement should be reached before the wedding as to the arrangements for in-church photography and it is worth mentioning that under copyright and performing rights legislation a fee is incurred if a video recording is undertaken inside the church. Regrettably, in recent years some guests and photographers have exceeded the bounds of decorum in what is after all an act of worship, forcing many ministers to set out guidelines that balance the taking of a good photographic record against intrusion. In many churches the flower arrangements will be undertaken by members of the church, but it is still another cost item. All these fees and donations should be paid well in advance of the wedding date.

The congregation burst into laughter as the minister at the wedding of a young man he knew well asked, 'Do you Susan take this Charlie . . .'
(Rev. Alex Cairns)

The structure of the **Church of Scotland** wedding service follows a set pattern. After the welcome and opening hymn, the minister makes a statement about Christian marriage. Then, following a prayer, the wedding vow is taken by both parties:

> I __ do take you ___ to be my wedded wife/husband; and do, in the presence of God and before this congregation, promise and covenant to be a loving, faithful and dutiful husband/wife unto you until God shall separate us by death.

After the taking of these vows, rings are given and received, with the minister repeating the lines:

> By this sign you take each other, to have and to hold from this day forward, for better, for worse; for richer, for poorer; in sickness and in health; to love and to cherish, till death do you part.

The **Roman Catholic Church** in Scotland also follows the same registration procedures. Thereafter, there are certain differences. For example, a pre-nuptial enquiry form must be completed by both parties as well as providing proof of baptism, confirmation and freedom to be married. And anyone intending to be married in the Catholic Church must attend a marriage preparation course. This usually takes place over four evenings, or it may be spread over two weekends.

Where both bride and groom are Catholic, the wedding service is an integral part of the Nuptial Mass. Where a couple wish to be married in a Catholic church but only one of the couple is of the Catholic faith, then a number of options are available. If a Catholic is to marry another Christian the couple can have either a Nuptial Mass or a wedding service, with or without Communion. If the Catholic party is to marry someone who is not a Christian, then normally there is a only a wedding service. If a Catholic marrying another Christian wishes to be married in the church of the other party, it is customary for permission to be obtained from the Catholic Church. Divorcees would be wise to consult with a Canon Lawyer if they wished to ascertain the possibility of marrying within the Catholic Church. Any priest would be able to advise of such a person.

There is one distinctive little ceremony which is worth mentioning relating to the presentation of a ring in the Catholic Church. The giver, starting with the thumb, touches the fingers in turn with the ring reciting in the name of the Father (thumb), the Son (index finger) and the Holy Spirit (middle finger). At Amen, the ring is then slipped onto the fourth finger.

While numerically smaller than the Church of Scotland and the Roman Catholic church, the **Episcopal Church of Scotland** provides the setting for many weddings every year. Divided into seven dioceses each headed by a bishop, the Episcopal Church is part of the worldwide Anglican Communion and as such has the authority to draw upon all the resources of that Communion, its liturgy and prayer books.

The Episcopal Church is sometimes seen as being halfway between Presbyterianism and Catholicism. For example, its stance on the marrying of divorcees is dependant on the decision of the bishop who will normally receive a recommendation from the local priest, and the wedding service may be followed, if desired, by the Eucharist. The conducting of the marriage ceremony outwith an Episcopal church also requires the permission of the diocese bishop. The order of service differs little from that of the Church of Scotland but the priest may devise their own framework and will seek to involve the couple to be married in the selecting of readings and the phrasing of their vows.

One rather nice ceremony encountered in the Episcopal Church is known as the lighting of the wedding candle. It is a symbolic gesture. After the closing hymn the bride and groom may each light a small candle before proceeding together towards the altar to light a large candle. They then return to extinguish their first candles, symbolising that there is now a new creation, that the two are now one. The large candle is given along with a Bible to the newly weds with the injunction to light it on wedding anniversaries to remind themselves of the vows taken on their wedding day.

Of course, Scotland is host to wedding ceremonies of many different religions, not just Christian, as well as to ceremonies of other branches of the Christian Church. Regrettably it is not possible to do justice to every wedding ceremony in a book of this length, but there are many publications available where further information can be found.

Your Wedding Venue

LOCAL CHURCHES, REGISTRARS' offices and hotels are likely to continue as the focal points for wedding ceremonies and receptions, and the strong feeling amongst many that only in a church can one really be married is recognised. However, an increasing number of couples are making use of the Church's willingness to officiate at a ceremony performed in an acceptable place – and the authority now given to registrars to carry out their function outwith their offices – to marry in a location possessing some special charm for them. You may like to consider the following:

THE NATIONAL TRUST FOR SCOTLAND

The style, splendour and diversity of the Trust's portfolio of properties is incomparable, with atmospheric locations available over much of Scotland. Over 80 properties ranging from castles to Highland estates and town houses are available. The part of the property to be used may depend on the size of the wedding and on offer are halls and ballrooms, libraries, drawing rooms, even restored old stables. Accommodation is also available in some places.

For properties mentioned here and other Trust properties, initial contact should be made with:

Corporate Hospitality and Events Department
The National Trust For Scotland
Wemyss House
28 Charlotte Square
Edinburgh EH2 4ET

Tel: 0131 9243 9405
Web site: www.nts.org.uk

Among the Trust's properties, the majestic Culzean Castle in Ayrshire takes pride of place as a wedding venue. Indeed, such is its popularity that more couples from England than Scotland get married there. Its appeal is also worldwide, with bookings including parties from America, Australia, France and Japan. In Central Scotland, Falkland Palace in the Kingdom of Fife holds pride of place for summer weddings, largely because of the palace's lovely gardens, a photographer's dream backdrop. In the North East one is almost spoilt for venues. Drum Castle with its 35-capacity chapel offers an exquisite setting in which to exchange vows, while Fyvie Castle with its gallery and tapestries almost belies description.

HISTORIC SCOTLAND

Historic Scotland owns and cares for many handsome properties and it is possible to have a wedding and reception at most of them. There can even be variations within one property. In Stirling Castle, for example, on offer are the Chapel Royal, the Great Hall, and the King's and Queen's apartments. Guest numbers need not be high for these venues. In the Gatehouse suite in Edinburgh Castle, for example, numbers are limited to 25. All properties being considered for a wedding should, of course, be visited well in advance of the wedding day.

To arrange viewing, contact:

Historic Scotland Functions Unit
Longmore House
Salisbury Place
Edinburgh

Tel: 0131 668 8686
Web site: www. historic-scotland.net

TOURIST INFORMATION

The many local Tourist Information Centres around Scotland are useful contact points. VisitScotland now provides general tourist information for the whole of Scotland. For information specific to weddings, visit their web site www.romantic-scotland.com. VisitScotland also provides a leaflet which includes water cruising contact addresses for those considering a waterborne ceremony and reception.

For those feeling the lure of Gretna Green and its Blacksmith's shop, contact the Gretna Museum and Tourist Services.

Other venues spring to mind, and not all historic buildings are held by agencies or trusts. Many clubs, such as the Royal Scots Club in Edinburgh, provide an ambience of interest, universities may open their chapels for weddings, and historic vessels such as the *Unicorn* in Dundee harbour are available. Even theatres now offer to host weddings. Many councils have halls or rooms with that certain something that seems right for a wedding. That there is an adventurous spirit abroad when it comes to arranging a wedding and reception venue is becoming more obvious. Budget and guest numbers must be your first considerations, however.

For general tourist information in Scotland, contact VisitScotland:

VisitScotland
23 Ravelston Terrace
Edinburgh EH4 3TP

Tel: 0131 332 2433
Web site: www.visitscotland.com (general tourist information and details of individual Tourist Information Centres), or www.romantic-scotland.com (for weddings).

If you are considering a wedding at Gretna's Blacksmith's shop, contact:

Gretna Museum and Tourist Services Ltd

Tel: 01461 338441
Web site: www.gretnagreen.com

or telephone the Registration Office on 01461 337648.

Invitations

THE INVITATION TO A WEDDING is normally issued by the family of the bride-to-be and in most cases will be the first notification of the event. While giving details of venue and times, the invitation serves a more subtle purpose; it tells something about the proposed character of the wedding. Is it to be a very formal affair, for example, or a slightly more unusual wedding? The design and wording used can set the tone.

Many stationers supply an abundance of cards, with various designs to choose from. Cards are also available in your chosen design for those only being invited to the evening reception, for the order of service, and sometimes for place cards.

Some stationers, and especially printers, will print cards with your own wording, or you can choose from one of two or three set ways of phrasing the invitation. Choosing your own wording is ideal if you want to set a particular tone, or if you wish to tell your guests something specific, such as special transport arrangements or dress; you may also like to include a map. Including all the necessary details will avoid further correspondence with the guests at a busy time.

Do be precise when describing locations. There may be more than one St Mary's Church in a town, and more than one wedding in progress at the same time in a stately home.

You may also like to consider custom-designed stationery for your wedding. Several designers offer this service, or perhaps you would like to design your own stationery or get a friend to do this for you. You can choose from special papers, hand-written inserts, or make use of your own computer.

Where a particular motif has been designed for the invitation, it is a nice touch if the motif is carried through to order of service cards and place cards.

The Best Man, Ushers & Bridesmaids

A WEDDING INVOLVES CONSIDERABLE organisation and although much goes on in advance behind the scenes, when the day arrives those carrying out specific roles will be under extra pressure. Long-term planning as to the numbers required to assist the bride and groom is essential. Much will depend on the number of guests expected; a small wedding in a registrar's office, for example, will obviously not require ushers on the scale of a large church event.

The Best Man

The best man is a vital ingredient in a successful wedding. True, eyes will focus on the bride and groom, but the best man is the staff officer, the man behind the scenes who carries responsibility for smoothness of operation on the day. He above all others requires an eye for detail, a nose for imagined or actual trouble. Because of his wide-ranging responsibilities, it makes sense for him to be involved in all the preparations from the start. He must, too, make every effort to establish good working relationships with everyone involved. Such paragons can be difficult to find, but hopefully cometh the day, cometh the man. The best man also needs to make a succcess the groom's stag party. If he is not likely to pass that test, the groom may wonder if he has the right man in mind.

Amongst his pleasant duties, the best man should consider giving thought to:

1. Meeting with the ushers to discuss the allocation of their duties, seating arrangements, who will walk out with whom, and so on.
2. Checking with the groom who has responsibility for collecting the necessary documentation (without which the wedding cannot go ahead) and when payment must be made, in the case of a church wedding, to the organist and so on.
3. Making the appropriate transport arrangements to the wedding and reception venues and verifying where guests are going to park their cars. Will umbrellas be required if it begins to rain?
4. Arranging buttonholes (perhaps even choosing them).
5. The wedding rings.
6. And what about those honeymoon flight tickets?

On the wedding day the groom may well be a nervous man. The best man will take responsibility for seeing that the groom is properly dressed, that any hired clothing is picked up in good time, that the temptation to have a drink (or more than one) is overcome, and generally make sure the groom knows what he is to do when he reaches the church. From this it will be obvious the best man should have gone over the arrangements with the minister at the rehearsal or arranged for time for this to be done before the service.

At a 'blackening' the groom-to-be was stripped naked, tarred and feathered and tied to a telegraph pole. His father drove by with a laugh without recognising him. A lady cyclist slowed down, looked and stared and continued on, commenting at home it had been an interesting cycle run. Fortunately the next to come along was a farmer's wife with a sense of compassion who untied him, took him home for a bath and sent him on his way wearing some clothes belonging to her husband.

(A ministerial story)

Immediately after the service the best man starts to win his spurs. He will make sure lost-looking guests know how to get to the reception, keep spirits up if the photographer is in never-never land, find seats for wilting elderly relatives and take action if the piper has disappeared or the paid-for-in-advance bells are not ringing.

It is at the reception that the best man raises his profile. Like a good host he will make sure that guests are introduced to each other and will intermingle with guests from both families. Some guests may arrive at the reception with gifts for the bride and groom and these have to be accommodated.

The best man will keep an eye on the catering arrangements, make sure guests know if their glasses should be filled at any particular time, and that the band know when they are due to play. He will also have had a word with friends about the couple's send-off, obtained confetti and arranged car decorations. He will be on his feet to read telegrams and messages, he may have to humorously ask for indulgence if a major mishap arises, and his reply to the toast to the bridesmaids will be eagerly awaited. His attention to the proceedings must not waver; it is his responsibility to make sure everything goes according to plan. And if a pay bar is in operation he had better make sure his wallet has a useful bulge!

The reception over and the guests away, the best man has some tidying up to do. The groom will have clothes to be collected, presents need to be dealt with and owners found for left-behind gloves and other articles. An exhausted bride's mother may have to be consoled. The best man, one hopes, will have risen to the occasion.

Ushers

Ushers are chosen from close friends and relatives of the bride and groom on both sides and their title well describes their main duty, which is to courteously escort the wedding guests to their seats. But ushers can make a considerable contribution to the overall success of a wedding and they should be assured as to what is expected of them.

The question of dress should be agreed with the bride and groom in plenty of time. The ushers should have an idea of the layout of the venue for the marriage ceremony. Come the day, the groom and best man will be ensconced in a vestry or like place and it is up to the ushers to make sure that all the guests can be escorted to their seats.

During the service it is the ushers who are on standby to deal with any emergency which may arise. Should a photographer be taking photographs of guests entering the church, an usher may have to liaise with him or her to name guests and give additional information when someone special such as the bride's mother is approaching. Ushers should also know in advance if any guests will need special help, if a wheelchair may be required, and where a carafe of water may be obtained in case the groom faints.

Ushers will also agree beforehand on 'who takes who'. Shall guests be welcomed by the ushers in rotation, or is it to be a case of the usher representing the bride or groom's side dealing with their own friends and relatives? They will make sure the front two or three rows are kept for close family members and friends and know which usher is to guide the bride's mother to her seat. How, where and when is an order of service to be handed out if one is being used? And should a guest arriving with an array of photo-graphic equipment be advised of any restrictions on photography?

Ushers should make sure they are fully aware of what is expected of them after all guests are seated and of the positions they should take up in both the processional and the recessional. After the ceremony, ushers will guide guests from the wedding place, help guests to their cars and verify that no bits and pieces have been left under seats. Once the bride, groom and best man have left the scene, it is the ushers' responsibility to tidy up.

At the reception the ushers have a role to play in circulating among the guests, especially mixing with guests from the other side. They may be required to phone for taxis at the end of the evening. Ushers have to have their wits about them.

Bridesmaids

When Prince Andrew married Sarah Ferguson there was not a bridesmaid in sight. For support, the bride was surrounded by flower girls and pages. I choose the word 'support' for, above all else, bridesmaids and matrons of honour, as their married counterparts are called, support the bride and help to make sure that everything runs smoothly.

Bridesmaids and matrons of honour are chosen by the bride from her close friends and relatives, and many brides like to choose a relative of their husband-to-be.

Some brides choose to have a show of presents before their wedding and bridesmaids will lend a hand. These are not always sedate affairs. In some parts of Scotland, Fife comes to mind, the showing of presents frequently becomes a part of what is known as a spree. While it is still an all-ladies affair, a small band may be brought in, and, following a meal and perhaps a toast to the bride by the chief bridesmaid, singing and dancing will be the order of the night. The jumping over a chamber pot holding salt is still practised.

On the day of the wedding, bridesmaids may lunch with the bride and her parents, help her to dress, and will normally travel independently of the bride to the place of the wedding.

In the processional, bridesmaids precede matrons of honour and the bride's attendants take up their allotted places at the front of the gathering. One bridesmaid should stand near the bride, ready to hold her bouquet and order of service as the ceremony progresses. There is an American custom that the chief attendant is responsible for carrying the ring the bride will give to the groom, but this has found little acceptance in Scotland, the best man still carrying that responsibility. After the service, the bridesmaids become part of the recessional, either paired with ushers or in step immediately behind the bride and groom.

At the reception, the bridesmaids will help to create the happy atmosphere by mixing with all the guests and keeping an eye on the bride to make sure she is never left on her own. They will also keep an eye on any flower girls or page boys in the wedding party and keep them occupied if their behaviour is wanting.

The Father of the Bride

Finally, a word about the bride's father. He forms part of the processional and, of course, 'gives the bride away'. At the reception, he will welcome the guests to the wedding, perhaps invite the minister to say grace, gives the toast to the newly weds, and should be ready to fund refreshments from his pocket. He should be in contact with the best man to ensure they are clear about who is doing what and when.

Transport

BRIDAL CAR COMPANIES CAN rise to the occasion with magnificent limousines for the bride and groom, but there is room for those who like to be unusual to make their mark. A horse-drawn carriage may be appropriate in some circumstances, as may be a vintage car. Or how about water-borne transport?

Whatever systems of transport are pursued, a logistical exercise inevitably follows. Let us stay with the traditional for a moment, whether it be the responsibility of a taxi or similar company, the best man or a nominated individual.

Arrangements ensuring the bridal party arrive at the church or other venue on time come first. The bride usually travels with her father. The bride's mother and bridesmaids will follow (either together or in convoy depending on numbers), this vehicle being earmarked for transporting the best man and bridesmaids to the reception or photograph location after the wedding.

The tying of shoes to a car dates back to the giving by the bride's father of a shoe to indicate a transfer of authority. The husband-to-be, though, had to give an assurance he would treat his wife well.

One decision to be made early on is whether to place the onus on guests to look after their own transport arrangements or to become actively involved with arranging transport for the less mobile or elderly and for groups travelling to the wedding from a distance. When drawing up the guest list, note those with transport problems to ascertain the depth of the problem, and those likely to have spare carrying capacity.

While it is easy to concentrate on transporting guests to the wedding and the reception it is almost as easy to forget the end-of-day arrangements. Have these been made? Do give consideration to organising a coach and obtaining special overnight terms at or near the reception venue.

After the wedding ceremony, at a minimum cars are required

for the bride and groom, best man and bridesmaids and the parents of the bride and groom. Verify the requirements of the minister if appropriate. It is sensible to nominate a responsible guest to stay behind after the wedding party has left to deal with any transport contingencies which may arise. This may involve carrying spare maps as to how to get to the reception, the parking of a spare car in case of a mechanical breakdown, taking over the wheel from Aunt Jane who is not feeling well and dealing with the hundred-and-one-things that can go wrong when one is not well prepared. And do ask the piper to keep playing after the bridal party has left to allow those still standing around to savour the atmosphere.

Many newly weds after the ceremony like to make their mark by leaving the wedding venue in a distinctive way. By helicopter is perhaps a little exotic but a vintage car creates an aura of the romantic. The nervy, though, will remember there is an old engine under the highly polished bonnet and not commit themselves to a journey of too many miles. A horse-drawn carriage is often popular and allows an unhindered view of the bride.

Finally, if photographs are to be taken at some park or country location, make sure the rendezvous point has been firmly identified. It is not good wedding practice to lose either the bride or the photographer.

Music

IT IS NOT SURPRISING THAT music figures so prominently in the wedding ceremony. Long before Romeo stood under a balcony in Verona and court minstrels strummed their lyres, love has been sustained by music. The couples must be few in number who do not have at least one piece of music they regard as 'their tune' and will remember the first time they heard it played.

But apart from this intimate association, love must surely be the dominant theme in the songs we live with and sing when we are happy or sad or in reflective mood. We think of courting to candlelight and soft music, recall robust wooing songs about distressed maidens and, succumbing to the lure of Hollywood, believe that songs of films from *Casablanca* to *Grease* were written with ourselves in mind. The live theatre too panders to our belief that love and music belong together. Would the Beatles have continued as a world phenomenon without such love songs to their credit as *Michelle* and *Yesterday*? Love and music are inextricable.

On special occasions we often seek the security of tradition. Most brides still come down the aisle to the strains of Wagner's *Bridal March* from *Lohengrin* as the guests sing 'here comes the bride' under their breath. But there are variations to this theme. Clarke's *Trumpet Voluntary* strongly sets the scene, while Bach's *Jesu Joy of Man's Desiring* finds favour with many. Recently, *Highland Cathedral*, played so dramatically by the band of the Black Watch as the British presence withdrew from Hong Kong, has entered the wedding charts, and a very lovely piece of music it is too. At the end of the ceremony, the triumphal strains of Mendelssohn's *Wedding March* continue in their popularity. Other options are available. Many couples turn to Handel, either his Minuet from his *Fireworks Music* or the Hornpipe from his *Water Music*.

There can be a lull in the proceedings while the newly weds are signing the register and this is a suitable time to include some music. If you are having a church ceremony, it can, of course, be left to the organist to provide the background to a conversation buzz, but some couples like to have a friend acknowledge the occasion with a song. The Lord's Prayer is a favourite but this interlude may be covered by anything from a love song to a special favourite of the newly weds. The singer, though, should have a good voice and be dependable. One organist tells the tale of a lady who had been celebrating slightly in advance of the service and who had no hesitation, or difficulty, in changing keys during her solo spot. The organist, unfortunately, did. Do not be surprised if a request to have a friend sing during the wedding is probed by the minister. A gentleman of the cloth tells the story of agreeing to marry a non-church-going couple in his church and nodding enthusiastically when the bride-to-be asked if a friend might sing during the service. Come the day and a shocked minister entered his church to see a karaoke unit installed where the service would be conducted. An alternative to the song is the reading of a favourite Biblical passage or a piece of poetry by a friend.

The fiddle and accordion are commonly used at Shetland weddings to lead the march to the church (which could be a six-mile trek in every kind of weather) with a gunner at the rear. It is a Shetland custom still kept alive, as is the fiddle playing.
(From Scotland's Music, John Purser)

As to the hymns in a religious ceremony, these are very much a personal thing. The twenty-third Psalm continues to lead the field, some of the more modern hymns are making an impact and *Amazing Grace* has its adherents. Other leading favourites are *Morning Has Broken, O Perfect Love, All Things Bright And Beautiful* and newcomer *Bind Us Together*.

The playing of the pipes as the newly weds leave the church always seems to bring an added touch of event. It is quite amazing how an instrument capable of expressing sadness can adjust to express celebration. Fortunately, with more and more people taking to the pipes these days, piper procurement is not a problem. Any local pipe band will be delighted to help. Remember, though, pipers do not play from music; they have their own repertoires which they carry in their heads and hearts. If you particularly want some special tunes, do give an early indication of these to the piper and be quite specific about when you want him or her to play. And make sure the piper is not going to be playing when in earshot of an organ or clarsach being played.

Yellow Pages (www.yell.com) and the Scottish Folk Directory (www.scottishfolkdirectory.com) list a number of groups available for weddings.

Guidance is also available from Blackfriars Music, 49 Blackfriars Street Edinburgh EH1 1NB

Alistair Cockburn, the administrator of the Clarsach Society, can be contacted at:

22 Durham Road South Edinburgh EH15 3PD

Tel: 0131 620 0904 Email: arco@globalnet.co.uk

At the reception, it is a nice touch to have some background music whilst guests are waiting to meet the bride and groom. And is there anything more appropriate to a Scottish wedding than the romantic playing of a clarsach? If procurement of a player is difficult, contact with the administrator of the Clarsach Society may be worthwhile.

Unless the reception is being held in a place with a well-known resident band such as Jim Macleod's in Forte Dunblane, a bit of thought will be necessary. A band that does not fit the company can lead to disaster. First, identify the kind of music that is sought: ceilidh dance music, country dance, a bit of ballroom dancing? Then give thought to other things, especially the decibel level. Do you want amplification? If so, how much? Is the requirement for a band that will run the show to their own agenda or must it respond to the ongoing directions of the best man? Word-of-mouth recommendations and inside knowledge are worth their weight in gold. If possible, hear the band in action before making the booking and verify that sufficient space is available for them where they are to be sited. With the equipment that some bands carry, a considerable area may be necessary. Do keep the hotel or appropriate staff advised of your proposed music arrangements. And it is worthwhile checking up on the dress the band adopts for engagements – there is something not quite right about well-turned-out guests dancing to a bunch of jean-clad musicians.

The dances that are appropriate for a Scottish wedding are dealt with in detail further on, but this is a suitable place to look at the first waltz, the dance led off by the newly married couple as the festivities get under way. At most weddings the dancing will not get under way until the meal and toasts have come to an end. If the situation allows it and the celebration is to take the form of a dinner-dance, the rather American form of the first dance following the first course of the meal can be appropriate, but make sure the kitchen is aware of the sequence being followed. One way or another, all eyes will focus on the bride and groom as, to a round of applause, they confidently or nervously, depending on the amount of practice they have put in, publicly exhibit how comfortable they are in each other's arms. After a few perambulations the chief bridesmaid and best man will also take the floor to be followed by the couple's parents, bride's mother dancing with the groom's father. Thereafter the company are at liberty to join them.

Flowers

IT GOES WITHOUT SAYING that flowers are very much part of the wedding. If not capable of projecting a personality they can certainly assist in the establishing of a mood from solemnity to happiness. Some thought, then, is warranted before one even crosses the florist's door as to the mood one wants to pervade where the wedding and reception are to take place.

Unfortunately, flowers even in high season can still be an expensive item and it is as well to recognise one's budget figure in good time. Be particular as to choice of florist. Seek out recommendations and ask florists for examples of their work. Ask questions, too, as to their total service, the making-up of bouquets, posies and table and church decorations and the transporting of flowers both to the place of the wedding ceremony and later to the reception.

Before going to the florists, make a specific journey to where the ceremony is to be held to verify what is available by way of stands and vases. If it is a church, ascertain if any other weddings are to be held around your wedding time that may have a bearing on your own floral arrangements. To what extent are you expected to leave your own arrangements in the church? Who will take down pew-end posies? There will probably be an established practice to which you will be expected to conform. In some churches there are congregational members who are willing to be involved in its decoration. If possible, take a back seat at other weddings in the church to see how others have approached this important facet of the wedding.

After the above research has been completed you can get down to choosing the flowers. Most quality florists will be happy to visit the wedding location with you to discuss things on the spot. But, at the very least, take along a sketch of the venue so that you can indicate where you would like the flowers to be sited. By all means, listen to what the florist has to say and after obtaining costings, discuss what flowers, foliages and colours are expected to be available at the time of the wedding to harmonise or contrast with the wedding outfits and the theme of your wedding. Remember, there is nothing wrong with seeking a quotation from more than one florist.

Photography

IT IS WORTHWHILE LOOKING at the wedding albums of friends and even those of vintage relatives to gather one's thoughts on how the great event should be recorded. Today, the photographer is a professional who holds a wedding prominence that would make yesteryear's photographer more than a little jealous. This is good; it can also be bad. It is good in that we now see greater thought going into a photograph, the positioning of the subject, the creation of interesting situations and especially the use that is being made of background. It is bad in that some brides and grooms leave too much to the photographer. A beautiful bride may look and be an exquisite picture by trailing branches at a trout stream. But does a husky Highlander really want to be reminded of his wedding by a photograph showing him staring pensively into the same stream? In other words, take the photographer into your confidence in good time.

Let him or her know how you want the special day to be recorded and with whom you want to be photographed. Do you want photographs of the bride getting ready in the morning and leaving for the ceremony? Some photographers are more than happy to take 'unposed' reportage-style photographs, if this is what you would like, at certain stages through the day. Consider, too, how long you wish the photographer to stay. Do you want professional photographs of your reception? There is, quite rightly, a relationship between work done and fee. Help the photographer to concentrate their attention where you want it. The moments you want recorded cannot be repeated after the wedding is over.

Most likely a local photographer will be used so it should not be difficult to obtain word-of-mouth comments as to suitability and effectiveness. See photographers in advance, examine their portfolios, and in particular decide which photographers you will feel most at ease with. Convey to them the kind of photograph you want to see on the mantelpiece after the event. Ask pointedly for best terms and special packages available, cost of reprints, how many copies have to be taken and so on. And please ascertain beforehand the licence the photographer may, or may not have, to move around the venue during the ceremony; the photographer's priority is to obtain the best photographs, not to sit as an admiring guest as vows are exchanged.

The wedding video, of course, has now come into its own and there are many budding amateur camerapeople keen to be in action. However, a video that flits from subject to subject without absorbing atmosphere soon attains comedy status. As with still photography, obtain the services of a professional with a reputation for producing the goods.

One of today's nice wedding touches is the presence on tables at the reception of disposable cameras. They provide merriment at the table and often produce the completely uninhibited photograph that one can look back on with affection.

Your Reception

THE RECEPTION MAY BE held in a variety of places and thought will be given to acceptable locations as regards travel, the bride and groom's attachment to an area or place, the size of room that will not be too big or too cramped for the attending numbers, car parking, and so on. But it is important to envisage the scene as it is expected to be. There is not, for example, much sense in booking a room on account of the view it offers if the reception is to take place in hours of darkness when curtains and lighting will be of greater importance. The old army adage 'time spent on reconnaissance is never wasted' springs to mind.

Unless guest numbers quickly rule it out, do not without thought dismiss the idea of holding the reception at home or in a marquee in the garden. There are outside caterers available who will competently take over the major reception chores for you.

An attractive venue for the reception having been identified, we now come down to examining the competence of the place to host the envisaged reception.

1. Does it have a good reputation?
2. Does it handle receptions for the proposed number on a regular basis?
3. Does the person you are discussing things with fill you with confidence?
4. Have you visited the cloakrooms to make sure they match the overall attractiveness of the place?
5. Is there a lingering smell of tobacco smoke?
6. Will overnight accommodation at a special rate be made available for guests unwilling to make a weary way home?
7. What if the weather encourages people to go outside?

Most venues dealing with wedding parties on a regular basis have developed a sequence that fits in with the size and layout of their rooms and their suggestions as to where and when the major toasts should be given and when the cake should be cut are worthy of attention. Should guests arrive at the venue before the bridal party (because it is still in the hands of the photographer, for example), make sure they are not left entirely to their own resources. They should be shown where to wait (with chairs for the elderly), hopefully there will be music, and give thought to the provision of a refreshment. In other words, make sure the reception does not get off to a bad start.

The Reception Line-up

While there has been a breakdown in formality at weddings over recent years, it is still much a part of the celebration that all guests are given the opportunity to pay their respects to the bride and groom and their parents. This can be done either by the bride and groom circulating around the reception or by a more formal line-up arrangement which at least ensures that everyone meets the bridal party. The groom, of course, is congratulated on his splendid choice of wife. The bride receives 'best wishes'. Some advice where a line-up is involved:

1. Make sure the guests have the option to be under cover as they wait to meet the wedding party.
2. Don't make the line any longer than it has to be.
3. Make sure someone is detailed to look after any gifts that may be brought to the wedding.
4. If the line is taking a long time to clear, there is nothing wrong in arranging for guests to circulate with a drink before meeting the wedding party, but do arrange a table where drinks can be deposited before these guests enter the line.

A good practice is for the bride's parents as the hosts to occupy the 'right of the line' position, the groom's parents standing next to them before guests meet the bride and groom. The best man, ever ready to smooth the operation, is on the bride's left and the bridesmaids may join the line or give valuable assistance by looking after guests, especially those who appear to be on their own. There are variations on this, but the one suggested does seem to result in less congestion and greater conviviality.

Food and Drink

The content of the meal itself is going to governed by cost. Caterers inevitably offer a series of priced menus for consideration and, not to put too fine a point on it, negotiation. The fewer the choices, the speedier the service to all. We have all been to functions where some finished their main course while others were awaiting the arrival of theirs.

Emphasising the Scottishness of the meal, the menu might be selected from the following (don't forget to cater for vegetarians):

Starter
Cock-a-leekie soup / smoked salmon and prawn parcels
Main course
Salmon / sea trout, or venison / Aberdeen Angus beef
Pudding
Crannachan / trifle
Cheese
Islay, Orkney, caboc

With regard to drinks, there is no substitute for the hosts giving thought to what their guests are likely to expect; most expect wine with their meal. Whether there should be a 'bubbly' or whisky/sherry toast at the outset will depend on the agreed plan and the budget.

Some guests will not be invited to the meal, only to the evening reception. Soup and sandwiches or nibbly things may suffice there. A pay bar is not unusual in the evening but no one will complain if they do not have to pay for their drinks.

The Cake

The cutting of the wedding cake is one of the focal traditions of the wedding. It is doubtful if many newly weds cutting the cake (jointly, to ensure fertility) realise the extended history behind the simple ceremony.

The tradition of a wedding cake can certainly be traced back to Roman times, when a confection, a mixture of fruit and nuts and sweet things, was put together as an expression of hoped-for fruitfulness and plenty. This mixture developed into small baked cakes which were thrown over the bride either after the ceremony or as she entered her new home. The use of small cakes seems to have been the custom for many years, with the French claiming the credit for two leaps forward. First, they added marzipan and sugar to the cakes, allowing them to be broken above the bride, the crumbling cake falling upon her. Later they sugared the small cakes together, allowing them to form one large centrepiece. In the nineteenth century came the innovation of a wedding cake of tiers, said to have been encouraged by the prolific church steeple-building programme of the time.

White with some pastel decoration is still the most popular colour for today's large cake although there are many startling exceptions. As guests will be keen to sample the cake, a calculation as to size is necessary. A rough guide for a traditional fruit cake is five portions to the pound, though an expert will be more precise, basing the calculation on the number attending the wedding and the actual content of the cake which will depend on the filling. As much forward notice as possible should be given when ordering a fruit cake, and bakers will consider two months less than adequate. When the baker removes the cake from the oven it will be drenched with brandy and the mix needs considerable time to mature.

Wedding cakes have gone through a considerable transformation, especially over the last 20 years or so. Thick tier pillars have given way to very slender ones and the American stacked, as opposed to tiered, cake is growing in popularity. No longer is fruit content *de rigeur*. Indeed, to some it is old-fashioned. Tier variation has become common: a three-tier cake may have a fruit base, a Madeira sponge middle tier and a chocolate sponge top tier. The outside coating has also changed, royal icing (a mixture of icing sugar and egg white) being phased out and replaced by sugar paste which is easier to work with and allows rounded edges in the design. Chocolate is also making an increasing contribution. Many couples nowadays like to design their own cakes, giving pointers to interests they share. Adornments may range from Elvis to racing cars or tartan, the cake colours often matching the bride's dress and flowers. Today's cake designers are producing some wonderful pieces of art and will be pleased to show examples of their past work and discuss the modelling of figures for the cake.

History, as we all know, repeats itself, and a central cake constructed from a proliferation of small cakes is starting to appear at many weddings, for example a tower built of meringues on trays (*croquembou* is the technical name for such a monument if it captures your imagination), or a pyramid constructed of profiteroles of different sizes.

Of course, if you wish to send out pieces of cake to friends or family who were unable to attend, fruit cake is the best option.

So far as the actual cutting of the cake is concerned, allow circumstances to dictate whether this is better done before the meal in an ante-room accompanied by a fairly quick toast or later in the dining room.

A final point: sometimes a friend is enthusiastic about making the cake. When this offer is accepted make sure the transport arrangements are all that they should be. A bashed cake is not a pretty sight and the camera, as they say, does not lie.

Seating Plans

Seating arrangements must be discussed beforehand. If most of the speeches are to be given in the dining room then a brief word with the main speakers will not go amiss. Some speakers are much more at home with the protection of a top table before them than in other situations.

The choices, then, are a top table with seating 'legs', a series of round tables for eight or ten, or a combination of a top table and round tables. With a top table a microphone can normally be installed more readily if required. Adopting round tables means that more guests will have to turn their chairs round to see the speakers, although many will endorse this layout as being more intimate.

Toasting – from an old French custom of placing a piece of bread in the bottom of a glass. A good toast involved drinking down to the bread.

Some would argue that more important than the siting of the tables is arranging 'who sits next to whom'. It is usual to mix the families at the tables, placing people with common interests within conversation distance of each other. Care, too, should be taken with singles. It is better they are mixed with couples and the occasional single rather than collectively be sent to Siberia with a table of their own.

Background music to a meal is always acceptable but it should be muted. There is a difference between pipes being played at a formal dinner (with a lament) and a happy wedding breakfast.

The main toasts and replies are normally enjoyed at the end of the meal when coffee has been served. Following the meal and toasts and perhaps a little break, it is time to take the floor. The celebrations are now under way

Finally, a comment on something that has been phased out over the last quarter century or so. A wedding at one time drew youngsters to the scene like a magnet. As cars left the church, car windows would be wound down and a handful or two of coins would be thrown out for luck, whereupon a free-for-all scramble or 'scrammy' for the coins would take place. Why did this happy if bruising custom die out?

Dressing
For Your Wedding Day
THE GROOM

Of the misbegotten changelings who call themselves men, and prate intolerably over dinner-table, I never saw one who seemed worthy to inspire love . . . About women I entertain a somewhat different opinion, but then, I have the misfortune to be a man.

On Falling in Love in *Virginibus Puerisque*
R.L. STEVENSON

Highland Dress

IT WAS IN THE AUGUST OF 1822 when what we still often refer to as Highland dress started its move centre stage to become the national dress of Scotland. The occasion was the visit to Edinburgh of the monarch George IV, when that portly gentleman, along with his subjects, succumbed to the panoply of tartan organised in honour of his visit by Scotland's greatest Lowlander, Sir Walter Scott. Scott, the father of the historical novel, was by this time introducing a reading public to the mysteries and legends of the Highlands, and had no compunctions about arraying himself in the Campbell tartan. J.G. Lockhart in his biography of Scott reminds us that the king was not to be outdone:

> The King at his first levee diverted many, by appearing in the full Highland garb, – the same brilliant Stuart tartans, so called, in which certainly no Stuart, except Prince Charles, had ever before presented himself in the saloons of Edinburgh.

The king's kilt, we learn from another source, was a little on the short side and his pink tights would find little support today. Lady Hamilton Dalrymple took the charitable view: 'since he is to be with us for so short a time, the more we see of him the better.'

Sir Walter's fascination with the Highlands extended to Highland dress. Cliff Hanley in his *Skinful of Scotch* suggests, in his inimitable style, one possible reason for Sir Walter's enthusiasm:

> He [Sir Walter] had seen the effect it could have on innocent strangers when he went to Paris during the occupation after Waterloo, and he noted that the 'singular dress of our Highlanders makes them particular objects of attention of the French'. I'll bet.

The Emperor of Russia was taken with the lads, too. At his particular request, a sergeant, a corporal and a private soldier of a Highland regiment paraded before him secretly at the Elysée palace, and the Emperor who had heard strange tales, achieved an ambition which is still nursed by nosey parkers all over the world today.

At home the British Government had recognised the psychological importance of Highland dress much earlier, by proscribing Highland dress in 1746 in an effort to eliminate warlike thoughts from the Gael after Culloden. The 1746 Act of Proscription, where the word kilt was formally recorded for the first time, had decreed that anyone wearing the plaid, filibeg, trews, or shoulder belts, tartans or particoloured stuffs, should be imprisoned six months for the first offence and, on second conviction, be transported for seven years. What other race was ever treated thus?

In the battle of Culloden, the Highlanders wore any tartan that came up their backs. They had never heard of the idea of an official clan design, and if they had, they would have dodged it because in these days advertising your name could easily get you a dirk between the ribs. The old clansmen recognised their friends in battle by wearing cockades or bits of feather or familiar expressions.

(From A Skinful of Scotch, Cliff Hanley)

Our Highland dress, of course, has a long history. The original covering of the Highland male was the Celtic *feile-breacan* or belted plaid. It was a piece of tartan cloth four yards long and two yards wide folded around the waist and held in position by a belt. The lower part fell to the knees and the upper part was drawn over the left shoulder leaving the right arm free for action. To attire himself in this substantial piece of material, an amount of dexterity was required. The plaid was laid out on the ground and the folds put in position before the Highlander lay on it, on his back, and buckled it on. As old books have pointed out, it was a dress for the warrior, the hunter and the shepherd. It could be lifted when crossing streams and movement was not restricted when climbing hills. When forced to spend a night in the open, the plaid would be dipped in water, the cloth would swell and the plaid became a windproof covering. In due course the upper and lower parts of the plaid would be separated, the *feile-breacan* now becoming the *feile-beag* and the lower part with its folds stitched eventually becoming the kilt.

The plaid, of course, as an item of dress was not to be ignored by the ladies, as Edmund Burt writing in the 1720s would point out:

> The plaid is the undress of the ladies; and to a genteel woman, who adjusts it with good air, is a becoming veil. It is made of silk or fine worsted, chequered with various lively colours; is brought over the head, and may hide or discover the face according to the wearer's fancy or occasion; it reaches the waist behind; one corner falls as low as the ankle on one side; the other part, in folds, hangs down from the opposite arm.

There are many descriptions of what constituted full Highland dress in the past, but two of the most succinct must be those written by James Boswell during his tour of the Highlands with Dr Johnson. First there was Malcolm Macleod of Raasay:

> He wore a pair of brogues, tartan hose which came up only near to his knees and left them bare, a purple camblet kilt, a black waistcoat, a short green cloth coat bound with gold cord, and a large blue bonnet with a gold thread button.

And then there was Flora Macdonald's husband:

> He had his tartan plaid thrown about him, a large blue bonnet with a knot of black ribband like a cockade, a brown short coat of a kind of duffil, a tartan waistcoat with gold buttons and gold buttonholes, a bluish philibeg, and tartan hose.

There is much of interest in these descriptions – the absence of white, the expressions of individuality – but especially that the referred-to dress was being described in the year 1773. At that time, the 1746 Act of Proscription forbidding the wearing of tartan had not been rescinded – there was another eight years to go before that happened. To these two prominent men, their native dress was essential to their comfort and well-being. The slight risk of being charged was worth taking. Today the wearing of our national dress still projects pride.

Shoes

The eighteenth century provides a range of quotations on early Highland footwear. Martin Martin in 1703 described the shoes then being worn as 'a piece of hide with the hair on' and, curiously enough, 'being tied behind and before.' Edmund Burt, the road-maker on General Wade's staff with an eye for the social life in the Highlands, acquaints us with the fact that 'pumps' is not a recent word and reminds us of the Highlanders' need for agility in a well-watered part of the country.

> . . . and are often barefoot, but some I have seen shod with a kind of pumps, made out of raw cowhide, with the hair turned outward, which being ill-made the wearer's foot looked something like those of a roughfooted hen or pigeon: these are called 'quarrants', and are not only offensive to the sight but intolerable to the smell of those who are near them.

And:

> By the way, they cut holes in their brogues, though new made, to let out the water, when they have far to go and rivers to pass: this they do to preserve their feet from galling.

The ghillie brogue or plain brogue is today's footwear, a lighter weight being the preference when the occasion demands dancing. The lightweight patent shoe with the buckle has allure and the considerable advantage that it blends with tartan trousers.

Those with country dancing as a hobby have made sure pumps can be found in some shoe shops. I confess I do not like them, and I am aware of a growing number of men, if not women, who find them a little too fragile for their feet. A more robust pump is now appearing, bearing the name, for what reason I do not know, of

Jazz shoes, and these have their supporters. But I have to add that only a short time ago I was at a village dance in Angus where all the men vigorously danced the full programme in everyday shoes.

When the ghillie brogue is being worn it seems to be the accepted custom in Central Scotland to tie laces round the leg, like some Viking warrior, with the knot at the front. Having done much of my early dancing in a glen where everyone tied the knot at the side, I still favour that practice and consider it in better taste. Laces around the ankle are not generally becoming to the female leg and drawstrings in pumps are to be favoured.

Stockings

How often one sees stockings pulled up almost over the knee, far removed from the Highland tradition, as the second line from the Gaelic bard emphasises:

> The pleated kilt is my delight,
> The hose that does not reach the knee,
> The chequered coat of varied hue,
> And the bonnet blue so cockily.

Any study of old Highland prints will show the stockings at calf length. Logan's book of 1845 with its illustrations based on original sketches is a good example. The best advice that can be given today on stocking height is to follow the old army adage of a hand's breadth below the knee. Again, old prints show the stockings to be finely knitted, showing off the line of the leg. It is a personal opinion that apart from the discomfort of dancing energetic reels with *élan* in thick stockings, many of today's knits, such as the Arran, remove elegance from the ballroom by giving the appearance of thickened legs.

Turning to the colour of stockings worn at social functions, one feels there is far too much emphasis on white, not a colour that found much favour with our male Highland ancestors. Claret, fawn or green frequently provide a more tasteful harmony or contrast than white. There is, after all, a fair Highland tradition that a man should do his own thing in the matter of dress. It is regrettable that dice-patterned stockings specially knitted to either match or contrast the colours of the kilt are now so prohibitive in price; and indeed one has to look hard to find a knitter with the necessary skills to turn out the elegant article. Castellated stocking tops are not often seen at weddings and with them the elegant *snaoim gartain* or garter knot. Garter-flashes that match the kilt are an attractive adjunct but the military-style green or red flashes are perfectly acceptable. An excess of material should not be shown and the flashes should be fitted centrally on the side of the leg, avoiding any bias towards the back of the leg

Finally on the matter of stockings, mention should be made of the *sgian dhu* worn on the outside of the leg of the right stocking, unless the wearer, of course, is left-handed. This 'black knife' was originally carried under the arm in a kind of hidden shoulder-holster arrangement, some claiming this was the Highlanders' way of beating the Act of Proscription ban on the carrying of weapons in the Highlands. Some years ago a properly dressed kilted figure was refused admittance to the House of Commons on the grounds he was carrying a weapon of offence in his stockings. The decision to refuse him admittance was formally challenged and the appeal upheld on the grounds the *sgian dhu* is part and parcel of Highland dress.

The Kilt

The most important part of Scottish national dress is, of course, the kilt, a form of wear with a long history. To begin with, our Highland ancestors' form of wear was, as already mentioned, the great plaid, and this in due course, with a little tailoring, became the philobeg.

Yet I suspect there were early variations on this theme. In the churchyard at Little Dunkeld in Perthshire is a very old stone on which Adam and Eve are represented in the Garden of Eden, the apple about to be plucked from the tree. Adam, be it noted, is wearing a kilt. Even making allowance for sculpting licence, it is a fair indication as to how long our ancestors considered the history of the kilt to be.

The proposed purchase of a kilt immediately raises the question of what tartan to wear. First, let us remember that although the kilt is essentially Highland in origin, tartan has much wider roots, some even claiming it as a Lowland invention. Certainly, the oldest piece of tartan that has been preserved (and it has been dated as third century) was unearthed in the lowland environs of Falkirk. It is interesting that our most famous weaver of tartan, Wilson of Bannockburn, who was certainly in business in 1720, operated south of the Highland line, and seems to have been allowed to weave tartan through the Proscription period in the Highlands. So, making allowance for the evolution of Lowland garb, which is as relevant to dress as anything else, I have always felt the case for incorporating tartan trousers into wear for special occasions to be entirely appropriate. Having said that, I will now await cries of wrath from certain quarters.

Before looking specifically at what tartan to wear, let us remember that the idea of a particular tartan being associated with a clan or name probably goes back only a matter of two hundred years or so, but that should be a long enough period for traditionalists. (In days of clan warfare it was the badge of the clan, such as a sprig of heath or fir, which identified membership and not a clan tartan.) However, we can imagine dyes made from neighbourhood plants coming to the fore in their localities, thus providing the origins of district tartans, noting again that many of these such as the Dundee and Musselburgh bear Lowland names, and it would be surprising if certain patterns or setts did not achieve a local appeal.

First choice for one's tartan is likely to be one's clan or family tartan and if this is not a straight relationship then some research might be pursued to see if a sept link to a clan exists. This can be a fascinating exercise. For example, it was a practice in the past for males to be being willing to change their surname, on marriage, to that of their wife, to ensure the continuance of her family name where its extinction was threatened, or where there was a financial inducement to do so. Failing in identifying a clan or family tartan, it is worthwhile looking at the District tartans where such links exist.

Politics, of course, need not be ignored: the Jacobite tartan was for those families that were 'out' in the '45 and the Black Watch for the government-orientated. The beautiful Caledonian tartan is another possibility, but a rummage through the sample books will show a wide range of unrecorded tartans that can be worn with confidence. Indeed, a kilt does not need a tartan. It can be of a plain colour such as worn by the London Scottish, while some Victorian landowners had a fondness for dressing their people in estate checks, but these lack the *élan* we are seeking for a wedding.

The kilt must not be worn too long otherwise it will look ungainly and will not swing properly when walking. As to length, the time-honoured way of getting the measurement right, which means the kilt must not cover the knee, is if when you are kneeling down the kilt does not rest on the floor. On that there is general agreement. An old piper remembers that in his regiment the gap between floor and kilt was reckoned by his pipe major to be the

breadth of two fingers, perhaps an inch-and-a-half. Other regiments would narrow that gap. Civilian kilts, of course, are pleated
to show the sett or tartan. It is only military kilts which show a
vertical stripe down each pleat. The London Scottish, being a law
unto themselves, wear the plain hodden grey.

Many tartans today are available in what is termed a 'hunting'
form where the louder
colours have been replaced
by more subdued colours.
Very attractive they are too,
although I wonder if sometimes the ladies wonder
what the men are intent on
hunting.

CUT KNEE CAP
IN HALF

HAND WIDTH
BELOW KNEE CAP

ABOVE LACE KNOT

TIED AT SIDE JUST
ABOVE ANKLE BONE

Now, a thought or two
on the use of white in tartans
and what we call dress kilts.
Queen Victoria, who was as
enthusiastic as they come
about Scotland and High-
land dress, is credited with
replacing white for red in
the groundwork of the Royal
Stewart tartan, still the tartan of our queen.

Inevitably weavers saw commercial possibilities and in due
course a range of tartans was woven, reaching the market with
the tag of Dress Gordon and so on. But where did the authenticity
come from? It is worth quoting Iain Taylor, always regarded as
highly authoritative on matters of dress, from his *Highland
Evening Fling*:

Queen Victoria, apart from her penchant for tartan curtains, had
known what she was doing, for her new tartan was in the tradition
of the old 'arisaid' setts for Highland women's head-shawls, plaids

and dresses. I am still doubtful if the male wearers realise the feminine source of these (dress) tartans.

Evolution in dress, as I have already said, is always with us and these dress tartans are popular with many males. But many may share the view that a white shirt, a prominent white on the kilt and white stockings all add up to too much white. A bride in white is one thing, but a groom in white?

Finally, when buying a kilt, give thought to the weight of cloth and the length of material it contains. Heavier wools have given way to finer worsteds. A measure of weight is required if the kilt is to remain at a dignified height while birling energetically.

The Kilt Jacket

Although most weddings take place during the day, it seems that many have decided that national dress means the wearing of evening dress, no doubt because that is when the festivities demand glamour should be at its highest. Watching a collection of kilt-clad males entering a church or garnishing the entrance to a registrar's office, certainly few tweed jackets will be on show.

The Argyll or Crail jacket, cut like a day jacket but in black barathea (a wool, silk and cotton mix) with which a tie can be worn, has always seemed to me a most appropriate wedding attire for an afternoon event. My impression is, however, that the 'Prince Charles' doublet leads the popularity stakes, complete with dress shirt and a bow tie that has hopefully been tied by hand. (If you find this difficult and a mirror less than helpful, practise first by tying the tie around the leg below the knee.) Not that Charles Edward Stuart ever wore such a jacket; like the other doublets that grace the scene nowadays, the dress top, and here I exclude the waist-length buttoned-up doublet, gives the impression of being descended from military wear. If the wearer is opposed to wearing a bow tie for a daytime wedding, then the Morar or Kenmore high-buttoned doublet with jabot (a frilled or ruffled piece of material worn round the neck) may be the answer.

Accessories

Kilt pins are an added extra, so to speak, neither right nor wrong. They should never be used to pin the upper and lower aprons together; that would eventually distort the hang of the kilt. As to the sporran, remember the kilt has no pockets and modern man has a lot to carry. I don't see even a small mobile phone fitting into a sporran (not yet anyway) along with the house and car keys, change and a few little extras. In other words, get a sporran with some capacity. Hairiness is not a sporran essential; seal or Arctic hare skin is eminently suitable. And make sure the sporran is not hanging too low. The sporran originated, of course, as a working pouch and is returning to what many claim was its original position on the belt as Jacobean-type shirts and waistcoats become more fashionable.

Trews

In my book *Highland Balls and Village Halls* I mention that the original form of trews, cut on the bias and leg-hugging, are just as authentic a form of Highland dress as the kilt but have little appeal today as a form of dress.

Made up of breeches and stockings all of one piece, trews, like the kilt, were forbidden by the Act of Proscription and never recovered their popularity after repeal. While mention of trews makes the name of Niel Gow the fiddler spring to mind, they were, according to Burt, an apparel of the better off, the chief mode of dress when a Highlander went to the Lowlands or anywhere on horseback. The tartan trousers referred to nowadays as trews and worn in Highland regiments are misnamed, but civilians were certainly wearing narrow tartan trousers in the early nineteenth century, as can be seen from such paintings as 'Sporting Meeting' and 'The Shamit Reel'. Outfitters' windows and the increasing appearance of tartan trousers at formal dinners prompt the suggestion that our national dress is not yet ready to resist evolution. Frock coats, too, have made their appearance. But as in all things appertaining to dress, good taste is the essential.

Highland Dress for Women

I will not become too involved in the important subject of women's wedding finery as this is dealt with in the following chapter by someone of much greater authority.

However, are ladies to be left behind in terms of national dress? Never have so many women been seen as members of pipe bands. Never have so many women been part of the ceilidh-dancing scene. Cannot the beautiful Aboyne dress or a variation of it evolve for these ladies? Even marching with men, it cannot be said the kilt is the most flattering wear for a woman, no matter how boldly they are playing the pipes. For some reason, on dress occasions ladies have been reluctant to bring the *tonnag* (shoulder shawl) or the tartan dress to the fore.

White, ivory or cream, which in many countries convey impressions of purity, are the most common colours of wedding dress today. It was not thus until a century or so ago. True, Queen Victoria got married in white way back in 1840, but she had a particular affection for the colour, as her later excursions into tartan design would show. Norwegian brides may adopt green on their wedding day while the Chinese may adopt red.

My daughter had the intention of wearing a sash of her family tartan as she entered the church on her wedding day, to leave after the ceremony proudly wearing a sash of her new husband's clan. Her courage seemed to fail her on the day, but I have always thought the idea had merit.

Dressing
For Your Wedding Day
THE BRIDE

BY JANE SMITH OF BELMONT BRIDAL STUDIOS

Her looks were like a flow'r in May,
Her smile was like a simmer morn;
She tripped by the banks of Earn,
As light's a bird upon a thorn.

Euphemia Murray
ROBERT BURNS

Choosing a Gown

DUCHESS SATINS, SUMPTUOUS silks, diaphanous organzas, brocades, damasks, devore velvets . . . there is more than a touch of the regal about the fabrics most associated with the today's bride which is showing no signs of changing. The wartime bride made do with her Sunday best suit, but the ethos is the same: a wedding means dressing up and today's bride has the freedom to choose how little, or how far, she wishes to express this.

Culturally we have come full circle back to the pre-Victorian days when a bride could wear any colour of gown. The white gown as a symbol of chastity is, save for the minority, at rest with its originator Queen Victoria. We are less concerned in today's predominantly secular culture with keeping up such traditions than with looking our best on the big day. After all, with the popularity of the wedding video, the bride can be a star for a day.

This isn't to suggest that wedding ceremonies and vows have lost their meaning, simply that the emphasis on the dress code has shifted from the symbolic to the romantic. Essentially this creates much more scope for interpreting the concept of being a bride: a leather-clad biker bride is as genuine in her intentions as a fairy princess bride, although, as with most things, the extremes are very much in the minority.

Designers now wield their influence on seasonal collections and trends more than ever before. For the past few years, boned sleeveless or strapless bodices matched with an A-line skirt have been extremely popular. Yet with the vast array of different fabrics, colours and finishing details available it is still possible to create an ensemble which expresses the individuality of the bride and her chosen theme. With many weddings taking place outwith the church setting, wearing a gown suitable for the venue, whether it be a castle, stately home or a beach, also plays a part. There is also the question of who pays for what. Nowadays many young couples contribute to the cost of their wedding and this will put restrictions on the gown, especially if their priority is a new home or an expensive honeymoon abroad. The couple may already have their own children, which may affect the style and budget. Whilst making the very best of her looks will be crucial to the bride, her final choice cannot be made without considering the wider context within which her wedding is taking place rather than traditional concerns. In simple terms, the great variety available to today's bride parallels the diversity of lifestyles and cultures we see in today's society.

While there is an incredible choice of over-the-counter and off-the-peg purchases, 'bridal' is still synonymous with bespoke services. Whether it is your gown, tiara or invitations, there is generally an opportunity to incorporate your own ideas in the finishing detail. Many brides-to-be find the

APRON-FRONT SKIRT AND
EMPIRE-LINE DRESS

enormous choice of bridalwear quite daunting, so where and how do you start searching for that dream gown?

As to the where, your best starting point is the *Yellow Pages*, or yell.com, their electronic equivalent. Here you can locate your local bridal stores. It is fun to take trips to, for example, London or Paris to try on gowns, but remember there are often at least two fittings required (and that's not withstanding any problems that do sometimes occur), so looking locally may be more practical. All the bridal stores in your area will have their own range of designers for gowns and by allocating stockists with a reasonable geographical distance between them, designs are sold on a limit-ed-edition basis. By checking adverts you'll see which labels each salon holds. If you have spotted a gown you love in a magazine, call up the designer or manufacturer (if their number isn't listed, just give the magazine a call and they should help you), then ask for the address of the nearest stockist to you. As well as retail establishments, most areas will have a choice of independent designers and tailors, so if you have a specific idea, you should approach them rather than the shops.

As with all things in life, there are advantages and disadvan-tages to approaching an independent designer, so here are a cou-ple of suggestions:

1. Ask a designer to show you a body of their work and give you references of previous customers. Every reputable designer will be happy to do this.
2. Remember that you will not be able to try on samples before you commit so it is a good idea to choose a style that reflects shapes that you know suit you, perhaps from your wardrobe. For example, do you have a favourite summer frock or evening dress?

Shops will not be pleased if you use their time and property (that is, their gowns) as a resource if you have already decided to get a dress made for you, and you must be wary of copyright laws.

Most bridal salons operate an appointment system as one-to-one attention is required and privacy is so important. There is no rigid formula for choosing a wedding gown; some people fall in love with the first gown they try on, others take a methodical approach, narrowing it down bit by bit. All brides are, however, in essence looking for the same thing: the gown that for them overcomes practical concerns and gives that intuitive sense of what feels right.

Remember, too, that this should be an enjoyable experience, a bit like the good old days when you sneaked into your Mum's wardrobe as a girl and appeared in feather boa, high heels and all. Try not to let the stress spoil the 'dressing up' fun. I always say to brides that although it can be excruciating making this big decision, your groom and guests are only seeing the gown you've chosen. Nobody is going to say, 'Oh, I liked that other frock better', and let's face it, everyone is on your side on the day, especially your groom. So go on, have a laugh.

The practical concerns are often a good place to start if you are struggling. For example, what shape of gown best enhances your figure? Be prepared for a few surprises with this aspect, keep an open mind and simply try on a gown from each of the main categories. Since the film *Four Weddings and a Funeral* I've heard 'I don't want a meringue' a hundred time! Beware: you may suit the fuller skirt and not all 'meringues' are over the top. Many are cut simply and elegantly (although it is safe to say that hoops are well and truly out and the softer effect netting achieves is far more flattering).

You'll get all sorts of advice on what ought to best suit your shape but you'll never be sure until you actually try on some dresses. Make sure that your salon has a large changing area with good lighting, plenty of mirrors and an experienced assistant to help you in and out of the gowns. Separates are an ideal way to test what shape of skirt and bodice suits you, then if you are certain you would prefer a one-piece gown it will be easier to track down the right combination. The main skirt shapes are *straight*, *full gathered*, *A-line* and *fishtail*. Necklines are generally *sweetheart*, *scoop*, *square*, *off-shoulder* or *slash*, which is a high cut from shoulder to shoulder. Currently popular is a soft *drape*, which suits lightweight fabrics, or a '*crumb catcher*' at the neckline. Dresses are quite simply a combination of these elements. Some other terms to know are *empire-line*, which refers to a gown that falls straight down from a seam under the bust, à la Josephine, and *princess-line*, which has the same under-bust seaming but flares out over the hips to a fuller skirt. In very general terms, princess line suits the figure with a neat bust but fuller hip, though please don't restrict yourself until you've tried all the shapes.

Choosing the right colour of fabric isn't easy either. There are so many shades of ivory since every fabric mix absorbs dye differently, so again back to my policy of trial and error. Many brides opt to have a colour assessment done before trying on gowns. Failing that, take along a good friend who will be honest (mothers and sisters generally excel in the honesty department!). A good idea when you are trying on gowns is to hold a bouquet of silk flowers in front of you to get a feel for the finished look; the colour this adds can often help to bring the ensemble to life. Gold and ivory remain popular since they suit a greater number of people than white, which can be quite a harsh colour albeit stunning on the raven-haired amongst us. Stronger colours like burgundy, blues, silvers and shell pinks also feature in most salons. My only advice with these gowns is to put some thought to what your bridesmaids could wear before you commit since you may be giving yourself a difficult task ahead. I wore red to my own wedding, so I'm all for giving it a go if you want to be different.

FULL SKIRT AND SWEETHEART NECKLINE FOR THE BRIDE, BODICE AND SKIRT FOR THE BRIDESMAID

The next part of the process is finding the gown that simply 'feels' right although you can't put your finger on why. In essence you are trying to express your inner personality through the gown. You are to wear the gown and not the other way around, as the saying goes. The experience of trying on a wedding gown often evokes memories of dressing up as a little girl and all the fantasies you explored as you were growing up and making sense of becoming a woman. Every one of us has our personal recollection of this, which is why so few women end up with exactly the same ensemble. I was obsessed as a girl with a Ladybird story book of Beauty and the Beast; I can to this day draw the gown Beauty wore and, save for the colour, I realised retrospectively that the style of my gown was the same (definitely a drama queen then!). Trust your intuition and ask yourself which side of yourself you wish to express: romantic, feminine, classical, traditional, modern? Do you want to be the fairytale bride or a classical Greek goddess? This is where you must stand firm against those who think they know you better than yourself; you'll regret not taking this chance as it will hopefully be your only one.

THE PRINCESS-LINE AND FISHTAIL

If you are planning a wedding with a particular theme, choosing may be made easier. One popular theme is 'medieval' with a castle venue. There are numerous gloriously embroidered bodices that suit this to perfection. For the bride choosing a Scottish theme, introducing tartan into your gown or those of your attendants is a consideration. Having seams piped in a contrast tartan works extremely well, or you could go for a tartan sash over the shoulder secured with a Celtic brooch. Tartan is woven in silk as well as lightweight wool so it is no problem if you want to have your whole gown made in tartan. I have seen a whole ensemble made with Black Watch tartan. The gown bodice was a dark green and the skirt Black Watch tartan with a riding-style hat trimmed with the tartan. The bridesmaids were in the dark green with sashes in Black Watch and the groom wore his trews in, yes, Black Watch. The whole thing looked stunning.

There are also designers that specialise in embroidery based on Celtic designs. The *Scottish Wedding Directory* will guide you to them.

Accessories

No wedding would seem complete without the flowers, church arrangements and bouquets in particular. Fresh flowers are no longer as popular as they used to be for decorating the bride's hair, having been replaced by the ubiquitous tiara. There are so many styles to choose from it is impossible to categorise them here. As with all things bridal, if you have a design you have created there are companies that specialise in making tiaras to order. Tiaras look good with or without a veil and are best tried on when you have had your hair done in the style you are thinking of having on your wedding day. My advice would be to arrange a hair trial then pop around the bridal shops until you find the right tiara. For those with flair, feather headdresses are also in vogue and can also be dyed to match your bridesmaids' dresses or your mother's outfit.

Local bridalwear directories can be a big help when it comes to choosing your gown and accessories.

Try **The Scottish Wedding Directory** *(www.scottishweddingdirectory.co.uk)* **or The Grampian Wedding Directory** *(www.grampian-wedding-dir.com)*

Veils were traditionally worn to hide the bride from evil spirits that may be lurking. In China a traditional bride wears a thick red satin veil and therefore must be escorted by her attendants up the aisle. At least with veils in this country you can still check that you are marrying the right man. Veils are still popular today, especially the long veils when a straighter style is worn. Again, the choice is huge. Please make sure that you try on veils with your gown as many people leave this to a later stage then find it is difficult to get the real picture when in jeans and coat. It is also essential to colour-match your gown and veil; that they both may be ivory is no guarantee they will be the same shade.

Bridal shoe manufacturers are finally taking on the issue that a bride wants to be comfortable as well as look good. It is hard to keep smiling at the end of a long day when your feet are killing you. Fashion victims beware: this is not the day for being crippled with pain. Most companies will dye shoes to a swatch of coloured fabric so that they match your bridesmaids and some companies offer to cover shoes in the fabric of your gown. This is pricey and subject to the fabric being suitable but worth considering if your shoes are going to be seen. For little ones the ballet pump style is still top of the list; best go for the one with the little bar over to avoid little feet slipping out. Unlike for gowns, you will find that for accessories there are a few specialist suppliers that crop up in many of the stores you will visit.

A Designer Gown

You can pay virtually anything for the gown of your dreams. The price reflects whether the gown has been manufactured to a standard size and style or whether it has been made to order to your individual measurements with design modifications.

Most designers who make individual gowns to order still use traditional methods of workmanship, hand-boning and beading. When you are buying a dress 'off the peg' do make sure that the alterations that you require are possible. Many salons offer an in-house alteration service, which is convenient; if not they should be able to advise you of someone local with bridal experience.

When you have chosen the gown you love, be 100 per cent sure since few retailers will return a deposit. Also make sure you know exactly what you are paying for:

1. Are alterations included in the price and if not what can you expect the extra to be?
2. How long will the gown take to come?
3. What if I lose weight?
4. When do I pay the balance?
5. What if the gown is faulty when it arrives?
6. Will you store the gown until my wedding?

Bridesmaids

Now, what about your bridesmaids? First piece of advice: wait until you have chosen your gown before hunting for bridesmaids' dresses. A surprising number of brides limit their own choices by doing this the other way around. It is a myth, however, that bridesmaids' dresses have to be exactly the same design, colour and shape as the bride's gown. This was fine in the days when confusing and confounding evil spirits was necessary but such superstitions don't prevail in today's society. The bridesmaids' dresses should essentially enhance your gown, picking out one feature (for example, the neckline or the skirt shape).

Popular colours are lilac and hyacinth for summer weddings and navy and burgundy for winter weddings. Gold and dark green were very popular a few years ago so must be due to come around again soon. I have seen a wedding party where each bridesmaid was in a strong, iridescent jewel colour (purple, red, emerald and gold). It looked fantastic, so don't be afraid to go with what you fancy. The only real considerations are your bridesmaids' hair colours (if you have a redhead and a blonde you will need to go for a colour that suits them both) and your desired flowers, bearing in mind that whatever colour your bridesmaid wears should appear in your bouquet.

Bridesmaids' dresses have changed in the time I have been in bridal from the puffy-sleeved frilly numbers to sleek, understated dresses in light, floaty fabrics. Bodices and skirts are also in vogue and have the advantage of being very wearable after the wedding for dances or parties. If you do have a group of bridesmaids where one is perhaps a good bit larger than the others, start by finding a flattering shape for her. Also go for darker colours and make sure that she is offered sleeves if she would prefer and a skirt with a slight flare since very straight skirts are really severe on anyone other than the tall and slim amongst us.

Again, it is no problem to get shoes dyed to match the bridesmaids' dresses, but a word of advice: please make sure your girls have all tried on the actual shoe they want dyed in ivory first. Sizing varies from company to company and most shops will exchange an ivory pair but once it is dyed you are stuck with it.

Little flower girls are still more traditional and fairy princess-like: little puff sleeves, a full tulle skirt, a bow – and a big sigh from your guests. Up to the age of about seven, depending on the individual child, this formula still works beautifully but remember thereafter that little girls want to be more grown up than this and you will have to source a dress that is a compromise between a child and adult style. Some companies do a teen version of the adult dresses which are ideal: they look grown up but don't have the bust shaping and have slightly higher-cut necklines.

Bridesmaids' duties include organising the hen night and now that I have been in bridal for six years I realise what a dull bore I am, my night out being a sedate dinner with some girlfriends! I shan't go into details but there is a wild element out there, so brides-to-be beware: choose your bridesmaids carefully (unless, of course, you are that wild child). The tradition of ritual humiliation of brides-to-be continues with everything from enforced fancy dress (veil, tiara and L-plates the most common) to making them carry a potty around touting for coins. In the old days the potty was filled with salt and coal but nowadays only money makes the world go round (I wonder if future brides-to-be will accept credit cards?). I have heard tales of forfeits that include the retrieval of male undergarments from some obliging soul minding his own business in the pub one minute who is assaulted by a 'henny' the next! All good innocent fun, though not from the bloke's point of view, I imagine. Other

DRAPE NECK

hen night accoutrements include the garter, wigs, fairy wands and a good doze of high spirits as well as spirits of the victual kind.

The garter, of course, is also a must for the bride on her day. How else will she get that photo of her groom removing it with his teeth? I think it is interesting that of all the bridal traditions that are upheld the fun ones are at the fore. The garter is a bit of harmless frivolity; the vows have been said and now it is party time. Most brides I know still believe in 'something borrowed, something blue'. The colour blue is associated with the Virgin Mary and therefore symbolises faithfulness and virtue. The borrowed item, usually a veil or piece of jewellery, brings good luck provided you are careful to borrow from someone within a happy marriage. Confetti is still thrown – originally it was grains of wheat or rice to symbolise fertility, now it is just for the sheer celebratory hell of it.

One last thing – time to present the bride with her lucky horseshoe. Keep it upright so the luck doesn't fall out, and now you can all go and enjoy the party.

Scottish Wedding Dances

When we first rade down Ettrick,
Our bridles were ringing, our hearts were dancing,
The waters were singing, the sun was glancing,
An' blithely our hearts rang out thegither,
As we brushed the dew frae the blooming heather,
When first we rade down Ettrick.

Ettrick
LADY JOHN SCOTT

Introduction

IN THE NATIONAL GALLERY in Edinburgh there is a painting that captures the atmosphere of a wedding. Painted by David Allan in 1780 and showing the wedding party and guests dancing the night away, it bears the caption 'A Highland Wedding at Blair Atholl' and is one of Scotland's earliest wedding paintings. As the guests gather today, making polite conversation and nursing their drouth while waiting for a photographer to complete his masterpieces of elegance and pomp, there is often the feeling that one mass action photograph is all that is required.

In Scotland, and here we vary much from our southern neighbours, a good wedding means good dance. And whether your normal taste is for shimmying or old-time, a wedding frolic demands a good share of Scotland's national dances.

In Scotland, dancing is in the blood and the following dances will get most people onto the floor. But remember that while there will be guests who know their dances, by the law of averages there will be some who are a bit rusty and may need a little help, and perhaps those for whom this will be their first dance. Give some thought to this; should there be a caller? If so, who will it be – band leader or knowledgeable guest? And don't forget to make use of the best man and the bridesmaids. Give them a dance refresher before the wedding if need be so that they can earn plaudits by helping guests on the floor. There is nothing unusual in a happy occasion needing a bit of forward planning.

If you are the bride or groom or one of their parents, make sure you can do a modern waltz with assurance. Traditionally it is the first dance and the eyes of the guests will be focused on you. However, let's make a start with the set dances (with descriptions and formation diagrams to help you out), the ones that get the party together.

Set Dances

DASHING WHITE SERGEANT

A 'round the room' dance in threes, a man being flanked by two ladies or the other way round but making up a dancing set of six. Half the groups of three will progress clockwise and half anti-clockwise.

BARS

1–8	All dance six hands round and back
9–12	Man or lady in centre of the three, sets to and turns the person on his or her right
13–16	Man or lady in centre of the three, sets to and turns the person on his or her left.
17–24	Each group of three on its own dances a reel of three (a local variation may be to swing each partner in turn)
25–28	Centre person joins hands with his or her partners and all advance to meet opposite group and retire
29–32	All advance once again and dance through opposite group ready to repeat the dance with the next group of three

THE EIGHTSOME REEL

Devised by the Duke of Atholl and some friends in the latter part of the nineteenth century, it is probably the dance for which Scots have the most affection, even if they can't do it. Form up in a square set, ladies on partner's right.

BARS

1–8	All circle eight hands round and back
9–12	Cartwheel clockwise, ladies joining right hands in the centre
13–16	Cartwheel anti-clockwise, men joining left hands in the centre
17–20	Set twice to partner
21–24	Swing partner or turn partner both hands
25–40	Grand chain (men moving anti-clockwise, ladies clockwise). Listen to the music and take your time (two steps to each hand back to original position); the dancing of this chain too quickly is a main reason for chaos ensuing in an eightsome
41–88	First lady goes into the centre and dances on her own while the remainder dance seven hands round and back
	First lady sets to her partner and turns him
	First lady sets to opposite man and turns him
	First lady and the two men she has set to and turned dance a reel of three across the dance
	First lady remains in the centre and dances on her own while remainder dance seven hands round and back
	First lady sets to the man on her partner's right and turns him
	First lady sets to man opposite and turns him
	First lady and the two men she has just set to and turned dance a reel of three across the dance

First lady returns to original place

89–232   The movements in bars 41 to 88 are now repeated in turn by second, third and fourth ladies

233–424   The movements in bars 41 to 88 are then repeated in turn by first, second, third and fourth men dancing with the appropriate ladies

425–464   Repeat bars 1 to 40

STRIP THE WILLOW (OR DROPS OF BRANDY)

This is another dance that can end in bedlam unless dancers listen to the music. Originally a weaving dance using a running step in 9/8 time, your band is likely to play a selection of Irish 6/8 jigs to make life easier for the guests who only dance occasionally. Although it can be danced in one long line (Orkney style) sets of four allow for more control.

BARS

1–4	First couple turn two and a half times right hand to finish facing second couple
5–6	First lady turns second man with left hand as partner moves into position down the dance
7–8	First lady turns partner right hand
9–12	First lady turns third man left hand and partner right hand
13–16	First lady turns fourth man left hand and partner right hand
17–28	It is now the turn of the man to work up the ladies' side of the dance, turning fourth, third and second lady in turn left hand and partner right hand
29–40	First couple now jointly work their way down the dance, turning each other right hands and second, third and fourth couples in turn left hands, finishing with the necessary turn at the bottom to return to own side

There are places where couples form up in one long line and the first couple commence after birling to work down the line as indicated in bars 29 to 40. After some progress has been made, the new top couple start dancing while the entire line moves up a place. Again after progress has been made, the next couple start dancing. There is little gentility attached to this variation of the dance.

VIRGINIA REEL

It might be difficult to prove that the Virginia Reel is of Scottish origin, but it is good fun and easily learned. The movements flow easily to a good selection of American hoedown tunes. The dance is best done in four-couple sets.

BARS	
1–8	Holding hands, the ladies and men twice advance in line and retire
9–24	All couples now do a series of movements: Turn partner right hand back to place Turn partner left hand back to place Turn partner both hands back to place Passing partner right shoulder, complete a do-si-do (back to back) And return to place
25–32	Joining both hands, top couple slip step down the set and back to position
33–36	Top couple cast off and followed by rest of set on their own sides, walk down to fourth couple position
37–40	Top couple join hands forming an arch while other couples dance up the set, the second couple now becoming the dancing couple

Set Dance Formations

LONGWISE SET
(for example, Strip the Willow, Virginia Reel)

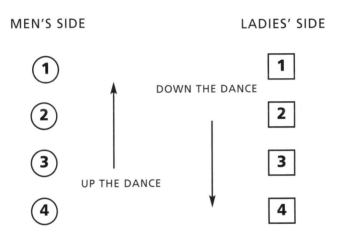

MUSIC

MEN'S SIDE   LADIES' SIDE

DOWN THE DANCE

UP THE DANCE

SQUARE SET
(for example, Eightsome Reel)

MUSIC

LADIES STAND ON PARTNER'S RIGHT

ROUND THE ROOM IN THREES
(for example, Dashing White Sergeant)

Couple Dances

OLD-TIME WALTZ

*Because of its importance, let's deal first with the old-time waltz.
It is in 3/4 time, that is we say to ourselves one-two-three, one-two-three as we listen to and keep in time to the music.*

In ballroom hold with partner, man takes a step with his left foot (1) then transfers weight to his right as it is brought into comfortable proximity to the left (2). He then transfers weight to his left (3) before making a step with his right foot (1). Left foot to proximity (2) and weight back to right foot (3). Then step left foot and so on. Once this fundamental has been mastered, it is easy to change direction simply by making the first step (1) at any angle.

SAINT BERNARD WALTZ

The couple start in a ballroom hold with the lady facing the centre of the room, the man facing outwards. The man starts with his left foot, the lady, who is going to follow his movements, starts with her right.

BARS

1–4	The man then steps gently to his left and closes right foot; steps again to the left and closes; steps again to the left, but this time, as the heels go down, they do so with some emphasis so that a distinct sound is heard in the room, the band frequently making a contribution
5–7	Man now reaches with his right foot to the side (lady following but with her left foot), closes, steps right again but this time as he closes with his left foot he allows it to smoothly move back a step before taking another step back with the right foot
8–12	Starting with his left foot, the man now takes two steps forward, the second step being of a half-left nature to accommodate his partner turning under his arm
13–16	Couple waltz round ready to start again

PRIDE OF ERIN WALTZ

Despite its name, this dance originated in Scotland. It is a most delightful dance.

BARS

1–8
Couples start facing the line of dance. The outside foot is pointed forward, then swung back, before dancing forward step-close-step to finish with a turn so facing against the line of dance. This is then repeated, the couple finishing in their original position

9–12
Now facing each other with hands joined, the man now crosses his left foot over his right foot before pointing his right foot to the side, the lady following but starting with her right foot over her left. This is now repeated in the other direction, the man this time putting right foot over left

13–16
Now we come to a part of the dance where there are local variations so do not be surprised if you are apparently doing something different. Turn away from each other and then return to face partner (some couples touch hands as they are back to back, others complete another turn). The main thing is to fill these four bars

17–24
With both hands joined, couple step towards each other and step apart before lady is turned under partner's left arm, so changing sides. This advance, retire and turn is then repeated back to own side

25–28
Returning to waltz hold, the lady now follows the man as he steps twice to his left along the line of dance and then twice to his right

28–32
The dance finishes with four bars of waltz

THE FRIENDLY WALTZ

A simple but useful dance for breaking down barriers in the early part of the evening. Joining hands, a large circle is formed round the room, lady on man's left. You may find distinct regional variations of this dance, so be warned.

BARS

1–4   Joining hands, whole circle swings in and out again. Man drops his hand from lady on his right, then guides lady on his left over to his right-hand side, the position now being vacant. All join hands

5–8   As before, whole circle swings in towards centre and out again. Man now releases lady on his left and helps lady on his right to face him. They acknowledge each other

9–12   In ballroom hold, couples take two steps to man's left and two steps to right

13–16   Couples waltz round, rejoining the large circle on the fourth bar finishing with man's partner on his right and smiling to lady on his left who will soon become his new partner as the dance is repeated

EVA THREE-STEP

BARS

1–2	Lady's left hand in man's right, facing line of dance, couple walk forward three steps and close
3–4	As dancers move in line of dance, man moves behind lady as couple take three steps to the opposite side
5–6	Man now crosses in front of lady as both take three steps to own side to rejoin hands
7–8	Couple walk back three steps and close, finishing facing each other in ballroom hold
9–12	Couple first step twice along the line of dance, closing after each step before taking a similar two steps against the line of dance
13–16	Dance finishes with four bars of waltz

BARN DANCE

There are two common forms of this popular dance which may be danced either as a couple dance, or, in a more friendly way, progressively with a new partner each time. To avoid chaos on the floor, announce in advance how it is to be done. The forms which may be used are known as the Canadian Barn Dance and the Highland Barn Dance. The difference is a matter of speed, the Highland form being faster, although I fear there is confusion about this in some quarters.

BARS

1–4	Couple proceed in line of dance with three steps to the music, finishing with a little hop, repeat moving backwards
5–8	Couple dance out to side three steps, clap, return to partner adopting ballroom hold
9–12	In line of dance continue step-close-step-hop. This step-close-step-hop is then repeated against the line of dance
13–16	Finish by rotating with a step-close-step-hop in the Highland form (the Canadian timing is more of a 1-2-3-pause). When the dance is being done in its progressive form, the move takes place during bars 4 to 8 after the clap, ladies moving back, men forward to meet them, new couple adopting ballroom hold to continue as in bars 9 to 12 above

HIGHLAND SCHOTTISCHE

To do this dance properly a knowledge of Highland Schottische setting is required. While standing on one foot, practise placing the other 'side-behind; side-in front' and implant the phrase in the mind. And one has to learn to make a little hop on one foot while extending the other leg. Where setting instructions are given they are for the man, the lady substituting left for right and right for left.

BARS

1–2   Couples face each other in ballroom hold for Highland Schottische setting. Hop right foot, point left foot to the side; hop right foot, left foot behind calf; hop right foot, point left foot to side; hop right foot; left foot in front of shin. Now, step to the left, close right foot, step to side left foot and, with a hop, bring right foot behind left leg

3–4   We are now to return to original position. Starting by extending our right foot to the side we complete our 'side-behind; side-in front', step to the right against the line of dance, close left foot, step to side right foot and, with a hop, bring left foot behind right leg

It is not as complicated in practice as it is on paper

5–6   Still in the same hold, man now steps to the left, closes right foot, steps again to the left while hopping on that foot, bringing right foot to calf. This is repeated back the way, that is, man steps to right, closes with left foot, steps again to right and while hopping brings left foot to calf

7–8   Dance finishes with four turning step-hops, lady often putting her hands on man's shoulders as he holds her waist

MILITARY TWO-STEP

BARS

1–4	Start side by side, lady on man's right, either nearer hands joined or man's arm round lady's waist while she places her left hand on his shoulder. In direction of dance, couple stretch outside foot forward to tap heel on floor before bringing foot back to tap toe on floor. Walk forward three steps, turning to face opposite direction on the fourth
5–7	Repeat the above against the line of dance
9–12	Couple face each other with hands joined. Man on left foot crosses his right foot over left with a kicking motion then returns right foot to position and performs a cross and kick with the left (variation of this is to set twice). Man now turns lady under his left arm
13–16	In ballroom hold, waltz round, opening up to repeat the dance

BOSTON TWO-STEP

This uses a setting step known as the pas de basque. *If this is new to you, practise doing your old-time waltz 1-2-3, putting your foot to the side on 1.*

BARS

1–4   Lady on man's right and holding hands, *pas de basque* out to own side and then in again. Walk forward three steps, turning on the fourth to oppose line of dance

5–8   Lady now on man's left, repeat the above setting out to the side and walking four steps

9–12   Couple face each other and set *pas de basque* twice. Lady does a solo turn to the right as man takes two steps to left to meet her

13–16   Couple waltz in ballroom hold

THE GAY GORDONS

A couple dance of somewhat indeterminate origin. Some claim it to have been named after a particularly flamboyant Duke of Gordon. Robbie Shepherd of Radio Scotland's Take the Floor *fame considers it to have developed from Scott Skinner's Gordon Highlanders March. Don't worry about its origins; it is an easy dance, good for including early in the programme because it encourages people onto the floor.*

BARS

1–8   In allemande hold, or, if you like, man's hand over lady's shoulder, right hands and left hands together, couple walk forward four steps and, keeping hands at the shoulder level, turn partner to face opposite direction while continuing another four steps backwards. This movement is then repeated, that is, four steps forward, a turn and continue in the same direction for another four steps

9–12   Retaining right hand hold, the man continues walking in the direction of the dance while the lady turns under her partner's right arm

13–16   Moving into a ballroom hold couple polka round, finishing ready to repeat

THE MODERN WALTZ

This follows the 1-2-3 pattern of the old-time waltz but is slower with a more flowing movement. As well as thinking 1-2-3, beginners might find it helpful to also think 'step-side-togethe; step-side-together'. Let's try it slowly, never mind the turns; if we can do it in a straight line we are almost there. I give the man's steps as the lady follows the man in ballroom dancing. She, of course, makes a left movement to the man's right step and vice versa.

EXERCISE A

Let's start by doing the dance in a straight line. Step forward left foot (1), weight on that foot as right is brought close by and placed a little to the right (2) and very slightly in advance of left. Close left foot to right (3). Now, step off with the right foot (1), bring the left close by, place a little to the side (2) and close (3). Repeat whole until competent.

EXERCISE B

Let's bend our straight line so that we can make the dance more interesting and avoid other couples on the floor. As you step off with either your left or right foot (1), angle your step away from the straight line of dance practised in Exercise A, but still bring your other foot close by the leading one as you place it slightly to the side (2). Practise until competent.

EXERCISE C

Now, if we can build in a little reverse turn, we shall not only be able to effortlessly turn at the corners of the room, but make our partner feel they have really had a dance worth remembering.

While we shall still count 1-2-3 we will now also say 'back-side-together'. The basic step is simple; let's do it in a straight line as we did in Exercise A. Step back with left foot, brush and side with right and close with left. Step back with right foot, brush and side with left and close with right. Practise until comfortable with this movement, then, as you did before, practise some retreating steps angled instead of straight.

EXERCISE D

The end is in sight. Let's put the forward and back together, practise two or three step-side-togethers to music, then a couple of reverse ones followed by one or two forward. And that is the modern waltz.

Appendices

APPENDIX I

The Marriage (Scotland) Act 1977

AT THE TIME OF WRITING, the most important piece of marriage legislation is the above Act which has repealed in whole or part some nineteen Acts dating from the Marriage Act of 1567. A considerable document (one might use the word hefty), its introduction was prompted by the increasing number of non-Church of Scotland religious marriages taking place in Scotland. The sections of the Act which may be seen in most major reference libraries are as follows:

1. Minimum age for marriage (no person domiciled in Scotland may marry before attaining the age of sixteen)
2. Forbidden degrees: relationships by consanguinity; by affinity; by adoption
3. Preliminaries to regular marriages: notice of intention to marry; loss of birth certificate; non-English language documents
4. Marriage notice book
5. Objections to marriage
6. Marriage schedules
7. Marriages outside Scotland where a party resides in Scotland
8. Persons who may solemnise marriage
9. Religious marriages: registration of nominated persons or celebrants (outwith Church of Scotland)
10. Removal of such celebrants from register
11. Alterations to above register
12. Temporary authorisation of celebrants
13. Preliminaries to solemnisation of religious marriages
14. Form of ceremony to be used by approved celebrant

15. Registration of all religious marriages
16. Registrar's power to require delivery of marriage schedule

Civil Marriages

17. Appointment of authorised registrars
18. Places at which civil marriages may be solemnised
19. Marriage ceremony and registration of marriage
20. Second marriage ceremony
21. Registration of irregular marriages
22. Interpreters at marriage ceremony
23. Cancellation of entry in register of marriages
24. Offences (falsification/forgery)
25. Regulations (power to make regulations under this Act requires Secretary of State approval)
26. Interpretations
27. Transitional and saving provision
28. Consequential amendments and repeals
29. Short title, commencement and extent

APPENDIX II

The Marriage (Scotland) Act 2002

THE DECLARED INTENT OF THIS act is to enable civil marriages to be solemnised in certain places approved by local authorities. This means that registrars are no longer confined to their offices when solemnising a marriage, as they were until the Act came into being. It should be noted, however, that the ceremony may only be carried out in an approved place. This approval is the prerogative of the local authority. In brief, should a party submit an application to be married in a certain location which is not regarded as approved by the local authority, an appeal may be lodged with the sheriff, though only on the following grounds:

1. That the local authority's decision was based on an error of law
2. That the local authority's decision was based on an incorrect material fact
3. That the local authority has acted contrary to natural justice
4. That the local authority has acted unreasonably in the exercise of its discretion

Such an appeal must be lodged with the sheriff clerk within 28 days of the date on which the local authority made the decision being appealed against. In upholding an appeal the sheriff may remit the case with reasons for his decision to the local authority for reconsideration of its decision, or reverse or modify the local authority's decision. The only appeal against a sheriff's decision is to the Court of Session and must be based on a point of law. Explanatory notes are available through Her Majesty's Stationery Office.

Suggested Wording for Invitations

TRADITIONALLY THE WORDING on a wedding invitation is very simple. It has to be clear who the invitation is from and to whom replies should be addressed. The place and timing of the wedding and details of the reception need to be given. If the invitation is for the evening festivities only, this should be made clear.

Here are two fairly standard examples:

> *Dr James and Mrs Elizabeth Sim*
> *request the pleasure of the company of*
>
>
> *at the marriage of their daughter*
> *Rosemary Alison Mary Sim*
> *with*
> *Mr Ronald Barr Johnson*
> *at St Michael's Church, Oban*
> *on Tuesday, 6 June 2002*
> *at 2.30 p.m.*
> *and afterwards at*
> *The Wallace Hotel, Oban*
>
> 7 Greater Road
> Oban
> EL89 7AY   R.S.V.P.

Dr James and Mrs Elizabeth Sim
request the pleasure of the company of

at an evening reception
to be held at
The Wallace Hotel, Oban
On Tuesday, 6 June 2002
at 7.30 p.m.
to celebrate the marriage of their daughter
Rosemary Alison Mary Sim
with
Mr Ronald Barr Johnson

17 Greater Road
Oban
EL89 7AY   R.S.V.P.

Advice on Speeches

WEDDINGS INEVITABLY MEAN toasts and speeches. To be given the opportunity of proposing a toast will be for some a pleasure, even an adventure, for others a frightening experience. There are many who enjoy getting to their feet, are accomplished in what they say, can tell a good story and get the party off to a good start and if such can be utilised it is sensible to make use of their talents. However, in many cases someone will be required to speak who does not possess these talents because, for example, he happens to be as the groom's brother serving as the best man and the family or others want him to speak. There are, as we all know, horses for courses, and it makes sense to use ministers, friends and relatives who are competent to be the major speakers, leaving the weaker as tail-enders. Books on public speaking are available for those who feel the need for them, but there are some general comments that can be made that are widely applicable to the less assured:

1. A wedding is a happy affair and guests will be supportive of the speaker, no matter how inexperienced he or she is.
2. When speaking, don't try to change your personality; be as natural as you can. You are speaking to receptive friends, not a gathering of parliamentarians.
3. There is nothing wrong in working from notes but start positively by knowing who has to be thanked for intro ducing you and how you are to address your audience.
4. If you can tell a story or you have a good story to tell – fine. Even if it is not all that funny someone is sure to split their sides. But be careful about crudity; what may be funny amongst young people may not have the same

appeal to older generations. In fact, stay away from any thing likely to cause embarrassment, even if there is a hilarious anecdote about an old girlfriend of the groom.

5. No matter what the toast or subject, the bride deserves a mention and flattery. It is her big day.

6. Prepare your speech in little blocks in a sequence that leads up to the toast. And practise, practise, practise – in front of the mirror or an understanding relative or friend. There is nothing like practice to produce a good performance on the day.

APPENDIX V

Suggestions for Readings and Speeches

IN A RELIGIOUS CEREMONY, particular attention should be given to the reading. The reading seems to produce one of those moments of silence when one can almost feel the minds being concentrated on what is being said. There are many readings to choose from. One of the most popular must be that taken from verse 4 of the thirteenth chapter of Saint Paul's First Letter to the Corinthians. The version in Lorimer's translation into Scots has a particular appeal to those with a love of the old tongue:

Luve is patientftu; luve is couthie an kind; luve is nane jailous; nane sprosie; nane bowdent wi pride; nane mislaired; nane hame-drauchtit; nane toustie; luve keeps nae nickstick o the wrangs it drees; finnds nae pleisur i the ill wark o ithers; is ay liftit up whan truith dings lies; kens ay tae keep a caum souch; is ey sweired tae misdout; ay houps the best; ay bides the warst.

Luve will ne'er fail. Prophecies, they s' een be by wi; tungs, they s' een devaul; knowledge, it is een been by wi. Aa our knowledge is hauflin; aa our prophesiein is hauflin: but when the perfyte is comed, the onperfyte will be by wi. In my bairn days, I hed the speech o a bairn, the mind o a bairn, the thochts o a bairn, but nou that I am grown manmuckle, I am throu wi aathing bairnlie. Nou we are like luikin in a mirror an seein aathing athraw, but then we s' luik aathing braid I the face. Now I ken aathing hauflinsweys, but than I will ken aathing as weill as God kens me.

In smaa: there is three thingsbides for ey: faith, howp, luve. But the grytest o the three is luve.

Further Bible readings worthy of consideration are:

1 Corinthians 13: 1–8	A favourite reading of many with its concentration (4–7) on the definition of love
John 2: 1–11	The story of the first miracle at the wedding at Cana
John 15: 9–12	Refers to the depth of love
1 John 4: 7–13	'Beloved, let us love one another'
1 John 3: 18–24	Gives the injunction to love in deed and truth
Ephesians 5: 1–2, 25–33	Not such a popular reading today, possibly because of its instruction that wives should obey their husbands
Romans 12: 1–2, 9–13	Practical advice on the Christian life

It is worth mentioning that although nearly all church wedding readings are drawn from the Bible, there are exceptions. A favourite is *On Marriage* from *The Prophet* by Khalil Gibran, from which this extract is taken:

Give your hearts, but not into each other's keeping.
For only the hand of Life can contain your hearts.
And stand together yet not too near together;
For the pillars of the temple stand apart,
And the oak tree and the cypress grow not in each other's shadow.

Shakespeare's love sonnets are other favourites. With some one hundred and fifty to chose from one is spoilt for choice. Sonnet 116 is a favourite of many, even at a Scottish wedding:

Let me not to the marriage of true minds
Admit impediments. Love is not love
Which alters when it alteration finds,
Or bends with the remover to remove;
O, no! it is an ever-fixed mark,
That looks on tempests and is never shaken;
It is the star to every wandering bark,
Whose worth's unknown, although his height be taken.
Love's not Time's fool, though rosy lips and cheeks
Within his bending sickle's compass come;
Love alters not with his brief hours and weeks,
But bears it outeven to the edge of doom.
If this be error and upon me provrd,
I never writ, nor no man ever loved.

The poems and quotations that follow may also provide you with material.

A Selection of Poems

Freedom and Love
T. CAMPBELL (1777–1844)

How delicious is the winning
Of a kiss at love's beginning,
When two mutual hearts are sighing
For the knot there's no untying!

Yet remember, 'midst our wooing,
Love has bliss, but Love has ruing;
Other smiles may make you fickle,
Tears for other charms may trickle.

Love he comes, and Love he tarries,
Just as fate or fancy carries;
Longest stays, when sorest chidden;
Laughs and flies, when press'd and bidden.

Bind the sea to slumber stilly,
Bind its odour to the lily,
ind the aspen ne'er to quiver,
Then bind Love to last for ever.

Love's a fire that needs renewal
Of fresh beauty for its fuel:
Love's wing moults when caged and captured,
Only free, he soars enraptured.

Can you keep the bee from ranging
Or the ringdove's neck from changing?
No! Nor fetter'd Love from dying
In the knot there's no untying.

O'er The Muir Amang The Heather

JEAN GLOVER (1758–1816)

Comin' through the craigs o' Kyle,
Amang the bonnie bloomin' heather,
There I met a bonnie lassie
Keepin' a' her flocks thegither.

Says I, my dear, where is thy hame?
In muir or dale, pray tell me whither?
Says she, I tent the fleecy flocks
That feed amang the bloomin' heather.

We laid us down upon a bank,
Sae warm and sunnie was the weather;
She left her flocks at large to rove
Amang the bonnie bloomin' heather.

She charmed my heart, and aye sinsyne
I couldna think on any ither;
By sea and sky! She shall be mine,
The bonnie lass amang the heather.

Kind Robin Lo'es Me
CAROLINA BARONESS NAIRNE (1766–1845)

Robin is my ain gudeman,
Now match him carlins, gin you can,
For ilk ane whitest thinks her swan,
But kind Robin lo'es me.

Robin he comes home at e'en
Wi' pleasure glancin' in his een,
He tells me a' he's heard and seen,
An' syne how he lo'es me.

There's some hae land and some hae gowd,
An' mair wad hae them gin they could,
But a' I wish o' warld's gude
Is Robin aye to lo'e me.

Extract from *Fy, Let Us A' To The Wedding*
JOANNA BAILLIE (1762–1861)

Fy, let us a' to the wedding,
For they will be lilting there;
For Jock's to be married to Maggy,
The lass wi' the gowden hair.

And then will come dancing and daffing,
And reeling and crossing o' han's,
Till even auld Lucky is laughing,
As back by the aumry she stan's.

Sic bobbing, and flinging and whirling,
While fiddlers are making their din;
And pipers are droning and skirling
As loud as the roar o' the lin.

Then fy, let us a' to the wedding,
For they will be lilting there;
For Jock's to be married to Maggie,
The lass wi' the gowden hair.

Fond Lovers in July
ALF T. MATHEWS (BORN 1856)

O Mary, will you marry me?
I canna live without you;
If I've to wait anither month,
I'll gae clean gyte about you.
I canna get a wink o' sleep,
For thinkin' on your charms;
To tell the truth, I'm never pleased
But when you're in my arms.

I wadna gie an hour o' this
For mansions or for money,
It's better than the promised land,
That flows wi' milk and honey.
Sic joys the rich man canna buy
Wi' gold at ony price;
O, when your head's laid on my breast,
Then I'm in Paradise.

And when I pree your rosy moo'
Still higher I maun soar;
The hot blood rushes through my veins,
And thrills me to the core;
And when I look into your e'en'
And see the love-licht there,
I seem to be at heaven's gate'
And you an angel fair.

And when I have your hand in mine,
And stroke your golden hair,
I seem to enter heaven itsel',
Withoot a single care.

I dinna care a snuff for meat
When you are by my side;
I feel that I could live in love
Frae Yule to Whitsunside.

I'll carry coals and hack the sticks,
And light the kitchen fire,
Gae tae the well and clean the boots –
In fact, I'll never tire.
A smile, a cuddle. Or a kiss
'll pay me for my pains;
Love disna bide in selfish hearts
That counts on greedy gains.

I'll strew your path wi' roses red,
And keep you snug and douce;
And I'll buy you a braw fur-cloak
Oot o' the London hoose.
My love's a love that winna dee,
A love that's ever true;
E'en bonnie Annie Laurie, dear
Was never loved like you.

You are the sunshine o' my life,
Frae you I canna bide;
Hae mercy Mary, or I fear,
I'll land in Sunnyside.
O, Mary, dinna say me nay,
An' fill my breast wi' anger;
For gudesake name the happy day,
I canna wait nae langer.

She Walks In Beauty

GEORGE GORDON, LORD BYRON (1788–1824)

She walks in beauty like the night
Of cloudless climes and starry skies,
And all that's best of dark and bright
Meet in her aspect and her eyes;
Thus mellowed to that tender light
Which heaven to gaudy day denies.

One shade the more, one ray the less,
Had half impaired the nameless grace
Which waves in every raven tress,
Or softly lightens o'er her face,
Where thoughts serenely sweet express
How pure, how dear their dwelling-place.

And on that cheek, and o'er that brow,
So soft, so calm, yet eloquent,
The smiles that win, the tints that glow,
But tell of days in goodness spent,
A mind at peace with all below,
A heart whose love is innocent!

Quotations by Scots

He that loves dearly, chides severely.

Love is as warm amongst cottars as courtiers.

Love overlooks many faults.

A man canna wive and thrive the same year.

Marry for love and work for siller.

Marry your son when you will, your daughter when you can.

There's ae guid wife in the warld, and ilka ane thinks he has her.

Follow love and it will flee,
Flee it, and it follows ye.

To marry is to domesticate the Recording angel.
R.L. STEVENSON

Oh! love, love, love
Love is but a dizziness,
It winna let a poor body
Gang aboot his bizziness
JAMES HOGG

Marriage is a wonderful invention – but then again, so is a bicycle repair kit.
BILLY CONNELLY

APPENDIX VI

The Church of Scotland Outside Scotland

THE SCOT IS AN INVETERATE traveller and there will be many who while wishing to enjoy a Church of Scotland wedding are unable to do so in the homeland. Fortunately there exists almost a world-wide network of Church of Scotland and partner churches offering an acceptable wedding service. Useful information is given below. There are, of course, in addition to the list given below, a host of Presbyterian churches throughout the world, not linked directly to the Church of Scotland, where the wedding service is not significantly different from that of the national church.

ENGLAND

St Columba's, Pont Street, London SW1 (linked with Newcastle St Andrews)
Crown Court, Covent Garden, London WC2
St Andrew's, Corby, Northamptonshire
St Ninian's, Corby, Northamptonshire
St Andrew's, Liverpool

CHANNEL ISLANDS

St Andrew's in the Grange, Guernsey
St Columba's, Jersey

CONGREGATIONS IN EUROPE

Belgium	St Andrew's Church, Chaussée de Vieurgat 18, B1050 Brussels
France	The Scots Kirk, 17 rue Bayard, 75008 Paris
Germany	Pauluskirche (City Centre), Bochum
Gibraltar	St Andrews Church, Governor's Parade

Hungary	Scottish Mission, Vorosmarty ulca 51, 1064 Budapest VI
Italy	St Andrew's Church, Via XX Settembre 7, 00187 Rome and Waldensian Church, Via s.Pio V 15 (first floor) 10125 Torino
Malta	St Andrew's Church, 210 Old Bakery, and South Street, Valetta
Nederlands	The English Reformed Church, Begijnhof 48, 1012 WV Amsterdam and The Scots International Church, Schiedamse Vest 121 (opposite eye hospital) 3012 BH Rotterdam
Portugal	St Andrew's Church, Rua de Amiaga, (opposite British Residency) 1200 Lisbon
Spain	St Andrew's Church, c/o Lux Mundi Ecumenical Centre, Calle Nueva 7, Fuengirola
Switzerland	The Calvin Auditoire, Place de la Taconnerie, (beside Cathedral of St Pierre), 1204 Geneva and St. Andrew's Church, Avenue de Rumine 26, 1005 Lausanne

The Church of Scotland also has entered into partnership arrangements with many churches throughout the world. Many of these partner churches are in Commonwealth countries or countries with historical links with Scotland, as shown by the frequent usage of Scottish names in their titles, for example, the St Andrew's Scots Memorial Church in Jerusalem and the Church of Scotland – Greyfriars-St Ann's in Trinidad. While the name of the national church only is shown below, it should be noted that many of these churches have widespread coverage within their own countries. The Church of Scotland will be happy to supply the name of the current contact individual in these churches. Contact should be made with the Board of World Mission of the Church at its office at 121 George Street, Edinburgh EH2 4YN. Telephone 0131 225 5722, or email world@cofscotland.org.uk.

PARTNER CHURCHES

Ghana	Evangelical Presbyterian Church
	Presbyterian Church of Ghana
Kenya	Presbyterian Church of East Africa
Malawi	Church of Central Africa Presbyterian
Mozambique	Igreja Evangelica de Cristo em Mocambique
Nigeria	Presbyterian Church of Nigeria
South Africa	Uniting Presbyterian Church in South Africa
Sudan	Presbyterian Church of the Sudan
Zambia	United Church of Zambia
	Church of Central Africa Presbyterian
Zimbabwe	Uniting Presbyterian Church in Southern Africa
	Church of Central Africa Presbyterian
Bangladesh	Church of Bangladesh
India	Church of South India
	Church of North India
Korea	The Presbyterian Church of Korea
	The Presbyterian Church of the Republic of Korea
Nepal	The United Mission to Nepal
Pakistan	Church of Pakistan
Sri Lanka	Presbytery of Lanka
Taiwan	The Presbyterian Church of Taiwan
Thailand	The Church of Christ in Thailand
Jamaica	The United Church in Jamaica and the Cayman Islands
Bahamas	Lucaya Presbyterian Church

Bermuda	The Church of Scotland Christ Church
Trinidad	Church of Scotland Greyfriars-St Ann's
Guyana	Presbytery of Guyana
Guatemala	National Presbyterian Church of Guatemala
	Maya Quiche Presbytery
Egypt	Synod of the Nile of the Evangelical Church of Egypt
	Coptic Evangelical Church
Israel, Palestine	Middle East Council of Churches
Lebanon	National Evangelical Synod of Syria and Lebanon
Cyprus	Middle East Council of Churches
Hungary	Hungarian Reformed Church
Portugal	Portuguese Evangelical Presbyterian Church

A Scots Wedding Service

THE FOLLOWING WEDDING service in Scots was translated by Rev. David Ogston, Minister at St John's Kirk, Perth, Scotland. He was approached by a young Scots couple wishing to be married with at least part of the service in their native tongue. Mr Ogston decided it was time to translate the whole wedding service into Scots.

The names Aileen and Michael are used throughout the version below, and this service includes David Ogston's own translation of the Twenty-Third Psalm and a song by Robert Burns. The scripture passages are quoted directly from W.L. Lorimer's translation of the New Testament.

This translation, along with *The Fower Sainins*, might hopefully stimulate regional variations. At the end there is an alternative suggestion for the wedding vows.

THE MERRIAGE SERVICE

Aileen an Michael hiv socht us here tae share this day wie them, this affset o their married life. An so we've come, fae hyne awa or near at haun, fae different hames and femmilies, tae wish them weel. Lat's aa be gled an lift a sang tae God.

THE TWENTY-THIRD PSALM O KING DAUVIT

My herd is the Lord, sae wants I hae neen,
I lie doon at ease in howes that are green.
Aside the saft souch o burns rinnin clean,
He leads me at peace.

My saul He restores again an again.
Wyes better tae tak He shows me tae ain,

For the sake o the richt an glorious name,
That is His aleen.

Though roch be the road an I traivel near
Tae mirk an meshanter, nocht wull I fear.
Close tee tae haun aye, Your stave is my fier,
My gledness an howp.

Faes tae the left o me, faes tae the richt,
I feast like a king, bi day or bi nicht.
Annointed an blythe an full'd wie delicht,
I nivver ging boss.

Lang as my days are, I trust in the poo'er
O mercy tae haud me safe an secure.
For I hae a bield faar walcome is sure,
The hoose o the Lord.

The Lord said, 'The Creator made them man and wuman fae the beginnin – for that cause sal a man leave his faither an his mither an haud til his wife, and the twa will become ane. Sae they are nae mair twa, but are ae flesh; and whit God hes jined, man maunna twine.'

Aileen, Michael – this is faat brings ye here – tae vow that you will haud een till ither come faat may. The vows you tak rax forrit tae the roads you hinna traivelled yet – tae the fowk you'll growe tae be faan life his vrocht its chynges – tae the bairns you'll hae, gin God gie ye that blissin. Here's foo the Bible picter's for's the length and breadth o siccan vows as yours:

Luve is patientftu; luve is couthie an kind; luve is nane jailous; nane sprosie; nane bowdent wi pride; nane mislaired; nane hamedrauchtit; nane toustie; luve keeps nae nickstick o the wrangs it drees; finnds nae pleisur i the ill wark o ithers; is ay liftit up whan truith dings lies; kens ay tae keep a caum souch; is ey sweired tae misdout; ay houps the best; ay bides the warst.

The pledge o luve as stieve as this luve, luve sae eident, is a leal an laistin pledge. Lat us speir noo God's blissin on Aileen and Michael as they mak ready tae tak their vows tull een anither. Lat us pray.

God an Faither, for this day an aa that this day means, we gie thanks tae You. We mind the lass fae Cana that bade Jesus an His kinsfowk tull her waddin feast; we mind foo Jesus set His blissin on them, an we speir that same blessin noo tae be on Aileen an on Michael.

Lord an Maister, for aa the wyes we growe an traivel forrit; for ilka mairch – dyke o experience, we gie thanks tae You. For aa the days that pinted Aileen and Michael tae this day – for aa the steps that led them tae staun afore You here – we gie You thanks. This is the day their coortin taks a tichter haud an faistens them till een anither; this is the turnin-pint faan they forhoo the bields that they hae kent, in order tae gyang furth themsels.

Jesus, King abeen an here aneth, grant faan they tak their vows till een anither, that they may be aefauld an honest nae juist for noo bit aa the time, so that their luve may aye be fae the hert and nae the teeth aleen. Sae lat it be.

THE QUESTION

Michael, wull you hae this lass Aileen tae be your waddit wife afore God an aa fowk, an wull you be hers alane, noo an aawyes?

I will

Aileen, wull you hae this man Michael tae be your waddit husband afore God an aa fowk, an wull you be his alane, noo an aawyes?

I will.

THE MERRIAGE VOWS

I, Michael, tak you, Aileen, tae be my waddit wife; I pledge you, in the sicht o God and aa the fowk that's here, my true an eident luve; I promise I will haud tae you an look efter you at aa times – weel-aff or in want – dwinin or hale and fere – till daith lowses me. This is my soothfast wird tae you.

I, Aileen, tak you, Michael, tae be my waddit husband; I pledge you, in the sicht o God and aa the fowk that's here, my true an eident luve; I promise I will haud tae you an look efter you at aa times – weel-aff or in want – dwinin or hale and fere – till daith lowses me. This is my soothfast wird tae you.

THE RINGS

This band is faistened wie these rings. Weer them for joy.

Afore God an his you twa hiv made your vows till een anither. Sae noo it faa's tae me tae cry you man and wife in the Name o God the Faither, God the Sin, and God the Holy Spirit.

The Lord bliss ye an keep ye. The Lord airt ye and gaird ye. The Lord hap ye wie His peace, this day an ilka day.

THE QUAICH

Aileen an Michael tak wine fae the quaich, an as they share this cup thegither they set doon the wye they will share their life thegither. (The bride is the first tae tak a drink fae the quaich – she passes it syne tae the groom. Naebody else drinks.)

THE FOWER SAININS

Een (the couple look straicht aheid)
The Lord bless tae ye the road that lies aheid: rax forrit yer hauns wie virr tae grup the gweed things God his in store for ye. The Lord be wie ye aawye on ilka path, kent or unkent.

Twa (the couple turn tae look at their guests)
The Lord bless tae ye the friens ye hiv already an the friens ye've yet tae meet.

Three (the couple turn tae their femmilies)
The Lord bless tae ye the femmilies ye come fae, an may He help ye tae ken in yer hairts the true an eident luve that his brocht ye tull this day. The Lord help ye te mak a hame thegither faar frien an ootlin alike will aye be welcome.

Fower (the couple look at een anither)
The Lord bless ye till ane anither; may He help ye tae luve ane anither wie a luve that's souple an swack.

God the First and Hinmaist haud ye ticht; His promises hansel ilka day an ilka sweet new mornin; God gie ye stieve hairts tae greet ilka challenge; God's peace be yours, His douce an haillsome peace, this day an for aye.

THE LORD'S PRAYER (SAID BI AA)

Faither o's aa, bidin abeen
Your name be halie;
Lat Your reign gyang forrit,
an Your will be deen here
as it's deen abeen.
Gie us oor breid this day.
Forgie the wrangs we've vrocht,
as we forgie the wrangs we dree.

Lat nae temptation pit's agley,
Bit keep us weel roadit.
For the Kingdom is Yours,
Yours the Micht an the Glorie,
Forivver an aye. Sae lat it be.

SONG

Gin a body meet a body,
Comin' thro' the rye;
Gin a body kiss a body
Need a body cry.
Ilka lassie has her laddie,
Nane they say hae I;
Yet a' the lads they smile at me,
When comin' thro' the rye.

Gin a body meet a body,
Comin' frae the well;
Gin a body kiss a body,
Need a body tell.
Ilka lassie has her laddie,
Ne'er a ane ha'e I;
But a' the lads they smile on me,
When comin' thro' the rye.

Gin a body meet a body,
Comin' frae the town;
Gin a body greet a body,
Need a body frown?
Ilka lassie has her laddie,
Nane they say ha'e I;
But a' the lads they lo'e me weel,
And what the waur am I.

Amang the train there is a swain
I dearly lo'e my sel;
But whaur his hame, or what his name,
I dinna care to tell.
Ilka lassie has her laddie,
Nane they say ha'e I;
But a' the lads they lo'e me weel,
And what the waur am I.

ROBERT BURNS

BENEDICTION

May the God o peace gaird the door o yer hoose an the doors o
yer herts. May the road rise tae meet ye, an the licht o the sun
staun at yer shooders. May the luve o God gaird ye and airt ye
aawye. Sae lat it be.

AN ALTERNATIVE FORM OF MARRIAGE VOW

In the Name abeen aa names, the Name o the Maist Hich King o
kings an Lord o lords, Chief o chiefs:

Dae you Michael (Aileen) in leal faith an eident purpose pledge
sair an siccar love tae this woman (man) Aileen (Michael) that
you will abide hand-fasted an truly buckled ane tae the ither in
the licht o aa suns tae come throwe dool an douce days alike?

APPENDIX VIII

Wedding Checklist

6–12 MONTHS PRIOR TO WEDDING

Decide on appropriate **budget**

Book official to preside over ceremony

Select and book **venues** for both wedding ceremony and
  reception

Set **wedding date**

Decide **number of guests**

Choose **caterer/wedding planner,** if required

Decide on **menu** for wedding meal and/or evening buffet
  (including special requirements)

Select and negotiate quantity and rates for **wine and
  champagne**

Select and order **wedding dress**

Choose and order dresses for **bridesmaids**

Interview and book **photographer** (and **video** if required)

Preview and book **musicians** for both ceremony and reception

Book **wedding-night accommodation** for bride and groom

4–6 MONTHS PRIOR TO WEDDING

Draw up **guest list** – divide into attendees of entire wedding and
  evening only

Order kilts and other necessary **male dress** from outfitters

Choose wedding **ring(s)**

Order **invitations** (and printing of order of service if required)

Book **honeymoon**

Estimate numbers and speak to hotel regarding rooms for guests
  who require **overnight accommodation**

Select **florist** and decide flower arrangements for bride, attendants
  (including buttonholes) and venue

Select **location for photographs**, if different from venue, and
  consider somewhere 'weather-proof' as an alternative

Book **transport** to and from the ceremony for wedding party

Book **hair/make-up trials** and final appointments

Decide on post-marriage **living arrangements**

Mothers should select their outfits

2–4 MONTHS PRIOR TO WEDDING

Send **wedding announcement** to local newspaper

Buy **accessories** for bridal party (shoes, tiara and so on), allowing
  time for dying of shoes if required

Buy **gifts** for attendants, if desired

Select and order **wedding cake**

Book **piper and organist**

Send out wedding invitations

1–2 MONTHS PRIOR TO WEDDING

Obtain **marriage licence**

Fittings of wedding dress and those of attendants

Decide **seating allocation**

Make final decisions on **readings and hymns** (if required) for the ceremony

Plan **rehearsal dinner,** if appropriate

FINAL PREPARATIONS

Confirm guest numbers for accommodation and for catering
purposes

Arrange any last-minute **beautician appointments**

Final dress fittings

Run through arrangements with wedding party and ensure that
everyone is aware of their responsibilities

FINAL CHECKS

Flowers (bride, bridesmaids, buttonholes, transport, ceremony, reception)

Transport (wedding party and guests)

Venue arrangements (including catering and accommodation)

Musicians (for ceremony and reception)

Photographer

Clothing (bride, groom and attendants)

Cake

Hair and make-up

Marriage documentation

Honeymoon arrangements

Further Reading

SOCIAL HISTORY

Bennet, Margaret, *Scottish Customs from Cradle to Grave* (Polygon)

Burt, Edmund, *Burt's Letters from the North of Scotland* (as related by Edmund Burt) (Birlinn)

Chambers, Robert, *Traditions of Edinburgh* (W&R Chambers)

Ganeri, Anita, *Wedding Days* (Evans Brothers)

Gavin, John, *Dowry Brides of St Cyrus* (Angus Council Cultural Services)

Gordon, Anne, *Candie For the Foundling* (Pentland Press Ltd)

Graham, Henry Grey, *Social Life of Scotland in the Eighteenth Century* (Adam and Charles Black)

Johnston, Tom, *History of the Working Classes in Scotland* (E.P. Publishing Ltd)

King, Margaret, various articles (Angus Council Cultural Services)

McGregor, Iona, *Getting Married in Scotland* (NMS Publishing)

Meigle SWRI, *Our Meigle* (Meigle Rural)

Pennant, Thomas, *A Tour of Scotland and Voyage to the Hebrides* (Birlinn)

MUSIC, DANCE AND DRESS

Dunbar, John Telfer, *The Costume of Scotland* (Batsford)

Emmerson, *Scotland Through Her Country Dances* (Galt House)

Hood, Evelyn M., *The Darling Diversion* (Collins)

Lockhart, G.W., *Highland Balls and Village Halls* (Luath Press Ltd)

Purser, John, *Scotland's Music* (Mainstream Publishing)

Shepherd, Robbie, *Let's Have a Ceilidh* (Canongate)

OFFICAL PUBLICATIONS

Marriage in Scotland (RM1) (from your local registration office
or New Register House)
Marriage (Scotland) Act 1997 (The Stationery Office)
Marriage (Scotland) Act 2000 (The Stationery Office)

Some other books published by **Luath Press**

ON THE TRAIL OF
On the Trail of Robert Service
G. Wallace Lockhart
0 946487 24 3 PB £7.99

On the Trail of William Wallace
David R. Ross
0 946487 47 2 PB £7.99

On the Trail of Mary Queen of Scots
Keith Cheetham
0 946487 50 2 PB £7.99

On the Trail of Robert Burns
John Cairney
0 946487 51 0 PB £7.99

On the Trail of Robert the Bruce
David R. Ross
0 946487 52 9 PB £7.99

On the Trail of John Muir
Cherry Good
0 946487 62 6 PB £7.99

On the Trail of Bonnie Prince Charlie
David R. Ross
0 946487 68 5 PB £7.99

On the Trail of Queen Victoria in the Highlands
Ian R Mitchell
0 946487 79 0 PB £7.99

On the Trail of the Pilgrim Fathers
Keith Cheetham
0 946487 83 9 PB £7.99

MUSIC AND DANCE
Fiddles and Folk
G. Wallace Lockhart
0 946487 38 3 PB £7.95

Highland Balls and Village Halls
G. Wallace Lockhart
0 946487 12 X PB £6.95

TRAVEL AND LEISURE
Die kleine Schottlandfibel
Hans-Walter Arends
0 946487 89 8 PB £8.99

Let's Explore Edinburgh Old Town
Anne Bruce English
0 946487 98 7 PB £4.99

Edinburgh's Historic Mile
Duncan Priddle
0 946487 97 9 PB £2.99

Pilgrims in the Rough: St Andrews beyond the 19th hole
Michael Tobert
0 946487 74 X PB £7.99

POETRY
Blind Harry's Wallace
William Hamilton of Gilbertfield
0 946487 43 X HB £15.00
0 946487 33 2 PB £8.99

Caledonian Cramboclink: verse, broad-sheets and in conversation
William Neill
0 946487 53 7 PB £8.99

Men and Beasts: wild men & tame animals
Val Gillies & Rebecca Marr
0 946487 92 8 PB £15.00

Poems to be read aloud
collected and with an introduction by
Stuart McHardy
0 946487 00 6 PB £5.00

Scots Poems to be read aloud
collectit an wi an innin by Stuart McHardy
0 946487 81 2 PB £5.00

The Luath Burns Companion
John Cairney
1 84282 000 1 PB £10.00

FOOD AND DRINK
Edinburgh and Leith Pub Guide
Stuart McHardy
0 946487 80 4 PB £4.95

The Whisky Muse
Collected and introduced by Robin Laing
Illustrated by Bob Dewar
0 946487 95 2 PB £12.99

GENEALOGY
Scottish Roots: a step-by-step guide to tracing your Scottish ancestors
Alwyn James
1 84282 007 9 PB £9.99

ISLANDS
Easdale, Belnahua Seil, & Luing & Seil: The Islands that Roofed the World
Mary Withall
0 946487 76 6 PB £4.99

Rum: Nature's Island
Magnus Magnusson
0 946487 32 4 PB £7.95

Luath Press Ltd

committed to publishing well written books worth reading

LUATH PRESS takes its name from Robert Burns, whose little collie Luath
(*Gael.*, swift or nimble) tripped up Jean Armour at a wedding and gave
him the chance to speak to the woman who was to be his wife and the
abiding love of his life. Burns called one of *The Twa Dogs* Luath
after Cuchullin's hunting dog in *Ossian's Fingal*. Luath
Press grew up in the heart of Burns country, and now
resides a few steps up the road from Burns' first
lodgings in Edinburgh's Royal Mile. Luath offers
you distinctive writing with a hint of unexpected
pleasures.

Most UK bookshops either carry our books in stock
or can order them for you. To order direct from us,
please send a £sterling cheque, postal order, international money order or your credit card details (number,
address of card holder and expiry date) to us at the address
below. Please add post and packing as follows: UK – £1.00
per delivery address; overseas surface mail – £2.50 per delivery address; overseas airmail – £3.50 for the first book to
each delivery address, plus £1.00 for each additional book
by airmail to the same address. If your order is a gift, we will
happily enclose your card or message at no extra charge.

ILLUSTRATION: IAN KELLAS

Luath Press Limited
543/2 Castlehill
The Royal Mile
Edinburgh
EH1 2ND
Scotland
Telephone: 0131 225 4326 (24 hours)
Fax: 0131 225 4324
Email: gavin.macdougall@luath.co.uk
Website: www.luath.co.uk